DATE DUE			

Our Endangered Earth

OTHER BOOKS BY JOHN LANGONE

BOMBED, BUZZED, SMASHED, OR . . . SOBER
A Book about Alcohol

DEAD END
A Book about Suicide

DEATH IS A NOUN
A View of the End of Life

GOODBYE TO BEDLAM
Understanding Mental Illness and Retardation

GROWING OLDER
What Young People Should Know about Aging

HUMAN ENGINEERING
Marvel or Menace?

LIFE AT THE BOTTOM
The People of Antarctica

LIKE, LOVE, LUST
A View of Sex and Sexuality

LONG LIFE
What We Know and Are Learning about the Aging Process

THORNY ISSUES
How Ethics and Morality Affect the Way We Live

VIOLENCE!
Our Fastest-Growing Public Health Problem

VITAL SIGNS
The Way We Die in America

Our Endangered
EARTH

What
We
Can
Do
to
Save
It

•

John Langone

Little, Brown and Company
Boston   Toronto   London

For Ray Desautels, my pal

First Edition

Library of Congress Cataloging-in-Publication Data

Langone, John, 1929–
    Our endangered earth : what we can do to save it / John Langone. — 1st ed.
        p.   cm.
    Includes index.
    Summary: Discusses the environmental crisis, focusing on such
    problems as overpopulation, the pollution of water, air, and land,
    ozone depletion, global warming, and disappearing wildlife. Suggests
    ways to improve life in the twenty-first century.
    ISBN 0-316-51415-2
    1. Pollution — Environmental aspects — Juvenile literature.
    2. Environmental protection — Juvenile literature. [1. Pollution.
    2. Environmental protection.]   I. Title.
    TD176.L36   1992
    363.7 — dc20   91-13763

10 9 8 7 6 5 4 3 2

MV-NY

Published simultaneously in Canada
by Little, Brown & Company (Canada) Limited

Printed in the United States of America

CONTENTS

Introduction
1
1 • Too Many Chemicals
5
2 • Too Much Noise
25
3 • Bad Air
28
4 • Dying Water
37
5 • Too Much Waste
56
6 • Radiation Pollution
91
7 • Too Much Heat
107
8 • Deforestation
116
9 • Threatened Wildlife
126
10 • Poverty and Overpopulation
151
11 • Energy
167
Notes
181
An Environmental Glossary
187
Index
191

INTRODUCTION

In the closing days of 1988, Pope John Paul II delivered an unusually harsh rebuke to the world. It came in a document, "Peace with God the Creator, Peace with All of Creation," the first papal pronouncement ever devoted entirely to the environment. In it the pope spared no one from responsibility for polluting the earth and the atmosphere and for ruining our natural resources. Our current attitude toward the environment, John Paul concluded, violates human rights and "lays bare the depth of man's moral crisis."[1]

The state of the earth is, or should be, of great concern to everyone these days. The media called 1988 the Year of the Environment, and 1990, which marked the twentieth anniversary of Earth Day, ushered in the decade now being referred to as the Decade of Environmental Protection.

Such attention is well deserved. As civilization fulfills its commitment to progress, that essential journey that is supposed to improve life, we sometimes abuse some very important things in our path — the air and water, trees and soil, and the wildlife that makes its home in these places. Regularly, we pollute the natural world with chemicals that kill plants and animals and endanger our own health. Our climate is being threatened; our energy resources are not only being squandered but are going up, literally, in choking smoke. Acid rain pours down on us, oil spills foul our oceans and beaches, and holes have formed in the earth's atmospheric shield that protects us from harmful radiation. We slash and burn precious rain forests and in doing so destroy life-forms that live there and nowhere else on earth and will never be seen again. At the same time, the world's population is exploding, and as it does, more and more people are contributing to the spoiling of the planet. And then there is the waste that piles up because of our careless ways, the rubbish of progress: dangerous radioactive waste from nuclear power plants, toxic chemical trash from our factories, and stinking garbage and sewage from our homes and businesses.

You already know of the more dramatic assaults on our environment. The Persian Gulf oil spill and the firing of Kuwaiti oil wells, the explosion at the Chernobyl nuclear power plant in the Soviet Union, the discharge of choking chemical fumes in Bhopal, India. But there are many others that you probably have missed — the 10,000 oil spills that have occurred since the Exxon *Valdez* went aground in Alaska, the pesticide contamination that sickens 300,000 U.S. farmers every year, the loss of 500 million acres of tree cover in America over the last twenty years, an area equal to the land east of the Mississippi River.

In the pages ahead, we will examine many environmental disasters, not only because they are timely but because the environment is one of the most important things for teenagers to know about. You, after all, have most certainly inherited the problems that plague the entire earth, and it will be up to you to deal with them in ways that, it is hoped, will go further than our current efforts.

It is the aim of this book to provide a balanced account of the specifics of the environmental crisis — how we got to where we are and why — and to offer possible solutions, or agendas for action, as they are now commonly called. We'll present these in a way that is designed to stimulate discussion; we won't attempt to offer any easy solutions. The ecological problems facing the world can be eased, if not erased in some cases, by taking certain steps. But there are no surefire remedies. Recycling, for example, is one way to deal with the nasty problem of waste accumulation — but it is not as easy as it sounds. Some materials do not recycle readily, the market for recycled goods needs to be improved, and, unfortunately, not everyone wants to recycle. Acid rain is blamed for the destruction of forests throughout the world, but scientists realize that other agents, including weather, plant diseases, and insects, are also culprits, and merely preventing the discharge of chemicals into the air may not be the only answer.

This book will also address the limits to what people can do to deal with environmental crises — limits created by the political, economic, and, yes, natural environmental changes and events that will always threaten to overwhelm any effort we make. We will argue that economic needs and a country's best interests must be balanced with the need to protect the environment, and we will emphasize the trade-offs, the compromises, that must be made if we are to clean up our environmental act. You will be asked to make decisions in each of the chapters. Should we, for instance, decide against building a dam that will provide electricity to people who need it if building the dam means we'll destroy a tiny, endangered fish's home? Should we ban chemicals that can ruin the environment even though those chemicals prevent the spread of plant disease and harmful insects? Should we stop burning coal because it is polluting and turn to nuclear power, which is also potentially dangerous? Do environmental activists have the right to use violence to block the construction of nuclear plants, the taking of whales, and the logging of trees? Should we require people to recycle their garbage? Which is worse, to incinerate all our rubbish or bury it in dumps? Should we prohibit our hospitals from using X-ray machines and other radioactive devices because the radiation is dangerous and adds to the piles of nuclear waste? Should we require people to have only a certain number of children so that there won't be as many people around to wreck the environment?

You'll also learn that not everyone agrees that we are really destroying the earth, or that nature will end one day, or that every warning environmentalists sound is true. All scientists do not agree that the greenhouse effect is ruining our climate, or that the environment is as fragile as it has been made out to be, or that it will not be able to readjust itself to pollution and deforestation. Not everyone agrees that waste is really a public health threat or that chemical companies and nuclear power advocates are all horrid, money-making destroyers of the world.

This book does not suggest that the problems of the environment are myths, and it does not water down the enormity of the crisis. But as each of the problems is addressed, please bear in mind that a realistic view of the current situation, based on knowledge of as many of the known facts and opinions currently in vogue as possible, is crucial. It would be far too easy to present a scary "death of the earth" picture in this book. That would be science fiction. Personally, I do not care much for such an extreme view, no more than I can accept the notion that all our energy needs will be solved by solar power and windmills and bicycles or that all our other environmental problems will be taken care of simply by saying, "Thou shalt not . . ."

One has to step back a bit — something that many of the more noisy environmentalists have been reluctant to do — and look carefully and, again, realistically, at the options. Simply to say, for instance, that we can wipe out carbon monoxide pollution by manufacturing electric automobiles is as simplistic as arguing that we'd all be better off if there were no pesticides, no nuclear energy, no loggers, no oil tankers, no garbage dumps, no incinerators.

Some of the solutions offered are, of course, obvious ones and may, indeed, be the only options, and we treat them as such when warranted. Some of the remedies that seem heaven-sent at first reveal their flaws when we examine them closely. Some may simply be impossible. By presenting all the options, however, by outlining the drawbacks and the benefits of each and by getting you to think them through, this book will enable you, it is hoped, to sift out the best approaches and come up with your own agenda.

1
THE PROBLEM:

TOO MANY CHEMICALS

We can't live without chemicals, but too often we can't live with them either. Chemicals, like nuclear energy, have sides as different as the familiar Greek masks of the theater — one smiling, the other downcast.

The use of chemicals goes back centuries. Primitive peoples learned how to tan leather with chemicals, how to ferment fruit juices and make just about everything from soap to paint. They knew how to extract various metals from rocks; steel was even made as far back as 3000 B.C. Eventually, chemistry moved out of the huts and caves of early society to laboratories, and then to industrial plants. Where once only small quantities of chemicals were used to produce some product or reaction, with the arrival of industrial chemistry, many tons — sometimes thousands of tons — of chemicals were now used.

On the plus side, chemicals and the chemists who work with them have made our lives healthier and more comfortable. They have given us drugs to treat and prevent disease, produced more and better food more easily, killed off swarms of insect pests, kept our floors polished, our clothes clean, our homes painted. Chemicals stop our fruit from turning brown, make potato chips greaseless, keep a car's radiator from boiling over in the summer and freezing in the winter, sweeten our drinks without calories, preserve our cold cuts, and give us substitutes for rubber and silk, cardboard and cotton, that Mother Nature could never have dreamed up. To get an idea of how important chemicals are in our daily life, take a look at the labels on the cleaning products in your house: sodium aluminosilicate and ethoxylated alcohol in your detergents, quaternary ammonium salts in your fabric softeners, titanium dioxide in a bar of soap, sodium bisulfite in toilet bowl cleaners, petrochemical distillates in furniture polish. The slogan of the Du Pont Company, a giant of the chemical products and explosives industry, is quite accurate: "Better things for better living, through chemistry."

But the statement is true only to a certain extent.

On the downside, a large number of the many thousands of chemicals on the market have done a lot to ruin our environment. Pesticides, for all the good they do, pollute earth, water, and air and can damage the nervous systems, livers, and kidneys of humans. It makes sense that because pesticides are designed to kill, they are among the most potentially dangerous of all chemicals. But they aren't the only villains. Food additives that we use to pickle our fish, color our fruits and beverages, and preserve our meats can cause cancer. When we administer antibiotics to cows to treat infection, we may contaminate their milk and perhaps make it unhealthy for some people to drink. The chemicals in plastics foul the air when plastics are burned, poison the groundwater when they leach out of landfills, and injure the workers who make plastics in factories. Mercury may be helpful in our thermometers and barometers, but it is harmful when it gets inside humans, fish, and animals. Rachel Carson, the scientist and writer who more than anyone else first alerted the world to the dangers of pesticides, put it aptly. "As crude a weapon as the cave man's club," she wrote in her landmark book, *Silent Spring*, "the chemical barrage has been hurled against the fabric of life."

While we hear a lot about chemicals today, they are certainly not new. They played an important part in the very beginning of life, in what is called chemical evolution. Scientists believe that the earth's primitive ocean was a chemical soup containing the key chemicals from which the first life would form. The theory is that lightning flashing through the original atmosphere changed particles of the gases methane and ammonia, present in the atmosphere at the time, into what are called amino acids. Amino acids are the chemical building blocks of protein, which is found in all living things. When the amino acids fell into the sea, they somehow combined there to form proteins.

Chemists have, in fact, duplicated in the laboratory what they believe went on in primitive atmosphere. As far back as the 1950s, scientists shot electricity through a mixture of water vapor, ammonia, and methane and produced amino acids. Later, other chemists did similar experiments and this time produced several of the chemicals that make up DNA, a "master acid" that controls the reproduction and heredity of every living thing from humans to microbes. DNA itself is made up of five chemicals — adenine, cytosine, guanine, thymine, and uracil. These five chemicals, called bases, spell out the genetic instructions for all life, but it is the way they are ordered and combined with other substances that makes a mouse, a man, or a mosquito. Scientists have even found these key chemicals that code genetic information in meteorites that have fallen to earth from outer space — leading to the speculation that chemical processes that create life are going on throughout the universe.

Just about everything we see around us is made up of only a hundred or so chemicals. Our bodies are constructed of chemical elements, including oxygen, hydrogen, and nitrogen, and various mineral salts such as calcium and sodium, and we need them all to survive. Just look at a bottle of multivitamin-multimineral pills if you want to see the names of some of the chemical elements and the organic compounds we call vitamins (they're also known as chemical regulators) that people take to maintain good health: thiamine (a B vitamin), pyridoxine (another B vitamin), ascorbic acid (vitamin C), zinc, potassium, manganese, chloride, chromium, selenium, nickel, iron, vanadium, even tin. Each chemical element, each mineral, each vitamin, has a special function in our bodies. The B vitamins, for example, promote growth, and vitamin C helps us heal wounds. Iron makes our blood red and allows it to carry oxygen. Zinc stimulates growth, and the small amounts of copper in our bodies help us use the iron properly. Some of the metals are even used to protect us against disease: gold salts may be used to treat arthritis, and manganese, chromium, and vanadium are said to protect against atherosclerosis, or hardening of the arteries.

Be aware, though, that many of these chemicals and elements that the body requires are needed only in small, or trace, amounts. Too much of any one of them — including vitamins — can cause serious problems, even death. Heavy doses of vitamin A and B_3 can damage the liver, and too much vitamin C can cause kidney and bladder problems. Chemicals that are not found naturally in the body and are not generally needed to keep our cells functioning — and this includes many of the common polluter chemicals and the heavy metals such as lead and mercury — can cause serious illness.

The following is a sampling of some of the most well-known toxic chemicals and elements, the ones that have captured the headlines in recent years and have done a lot of damage to our fragile environment. They, and others, will be discussed in more detail a bit later when we consider the different environmental hazards, but it is a good idea to familiarize yourself with some of them before reading ahead, because they are the pollutants that government, industry, and the general public have been most concerned about.

AGENT ORANGE

This chemical mixture is a defoliant, a substance used to force plants and trees to lose their leaves. The U.S. Army sprayed it over the jungles during the Vietnam War to strip them bare so that the enemy could be seen more easily. Agent Orange has also been used by farmers and cattle ranchers to kill weeds and brush.

Agent Orange, like many agricultural chemicals, contains toxic substances, among them one we'll discuss later in our list, dioxin.

Although Agent Orange has a legitimate use, it can be dangerous to humans. After the Vietnam War, tens of thousands of veterans — American and North Vietnamese — who were exposed to the chemical said they had experienced headaches, stomach and nervous system disorders, psychological changes, and cancer. There were also claims that some veterans who had been near Agent Orange had fathered deformed children.

Opinions still differ widely over whether Agent Orange was responsible for many of the physical and mental disorders the veterans experienced. One Air Force study found, in fact, that there were fewer incidences of cancer among the airmen directly involved in spraying the chemical than in the civilian population in general. But because the amount of Agent Orange used by the military was reportedly at least three times higher than what is used by farmers — and also used undiluted, which is not the case among civilian users — the concern is understandable, given what we know about the toxicity of pesticides and herbicides.

ALAR

A trade name for the chemical daminozide, Alar was sprayed on apples to make them ripen at the same time so they could be harvested all at once, and to make them firm and colorful.

Alar serves as a good example of what can happen when environmentalists and the chemical industry clash, as well as an example of how to weigh the risk of a chemical against its benefit.

In January 1989, the U.S. Environmental Protection Agency (EPA) raised the possibility that people who ate apples treated with Alar could be at risk for cancer. The EPA did not consider the evidence strong enough to declare a health emergency, however, so the chemical was not banned. Then, after a national television program reported on a study by an environmental group that Alar was a special hazard to children — who eat more apples and drink more apple products for their size than adults do — consumers became alarmed and stopped buying apples.

Responding to the concern, the chemical's manufacturer voluntarily removed it from the market. The apple industry also announced it would stop using it — even though to do so would cost the growers many millions of dollars for the year because without Alar it would take longer to pick their crops and because people might not buy apples that were not as red or as crisp as they might have been if they had been sprayed.

As it turned out, the apple crop was tasty anyway, even though a bit smaller, and first reports indicated that sales were not adversely affected. One orchard owner summed up the flap this way:

> Arguments on all sides reached an emotional level that precluded good judgment. Everybody got scared, including the people who started it. The environmentalists didn't mean to have such a devastating effect on the apple community. Nobody played it very well. It was like a religious disagreement.[1]

About a year later, a group of apple growers filed a lawsuit against the television network and the environmental group that had singled out Alar. The suit contended that apple growers had lost millions of dollars in sales because of the program.

Think a bit about the Alar case. Should the growers have stopped using the chemical on evidence that was not strong? Were the environmentalists right in alarming the public? What good, if any, may come out of the Alar controversy?

ARSENIC

Arsenic is a silver-gray element that has many forms, some of which are used in small amounts in medicines, hair dyes, and various hair tonics. One form is arsenic trioxide, a very toxic, white, odorless compound that is a prime ingredient of insecticides, herbicides, and rat killers. This compound is also used in pigments and wood preservatives and to remove the color from glass. It may also cause cancer.

Arsenic poisoning is not uncommon and occurs chiefly in people who work with the chemical or who live in areas where arsenic pollutes the air around factories and mines. When farmers use arsenic, it stays in the ground and sometimes gets into groundwater supplies, fruit juices, and wines. Always read the labels of any pesticides or herbicides you might use, and if they contain arsenic, either look for a substitute or be very careful how you use them.

ASBESTOS

Asbestos, a fibrous mineral found in nature, has many commercial uses. Its name comes from a Greek word meaning unquenchable, an appropriate name because asbestos is resistant to heat and acid. It is also very strong and light. For those reasons, asbestos is often used to make fireproof clothing and other fire-resistant materials and to insulate electrical equipment. Thousands of products that are used every day contain some asbestos. It is in brake linings for cars and trains, roofing materials, and ironing board covers. Asbestos insulates our homes, schools, and office buildings, as well as the steam boilers and hot-water pipes inside them. It is used in filters that screen out contaminants during the manufacture of soft drinks, beer, and liquor.

There is no question that asbestos is valuable and that without it modern society would have a difficult time going about its daily activities. For this reason, and because reliable substitutes are not available, asbestos will continue to be used throughout the world for some time to come.

But asbestos can be hazardous to our health when we inhale its dust and fibers. This can happen when workers are exposed to asbestos in mines or in factories that either process the mineral or use it to make asbestos products. Workers also may breathe in asbestos when they are tearing down or renovating buildings, repairing old furnaces, or replacing automobile brake linings. Firefighters who prowl through burned-out buildings are also exposed to asbestos dust and fibers. Because asbestos is so widely used and because it is released into the air, we all may be exposed to some amount of it — at home, at work, or in school.

As is the case with cigarette smoke, the biggest health risk from asbestos exposure is lung disease. One of the diseases for which it can be responsible is asbestosis, which causes severe breathing difficulties. Other asbestos-related diseases are mesothelioma, a rare and fatal cancer of the lungs, and stomach cancer. Families of asbestos workers are also at risk because the clothes the workers wear home are often full of the poisonous dust. As has happened with Agent Orange, thousands of former asbestos workers all over the country have sued asbestos companies for damaging their health.

There are now strong regulations about how much asbestos dust can be present in the air of factories. Protective equipment and ventilating systems that cleanse the air of dust are used in the factories, and when workers demolish buildings there are rules about how to first remove the asbestos-coated materials safely. Every time a wall that has been insulated with asbestos is dropped from a building, dust will arise, and construction workers usually lower the walls carefully to the ground or wrap them in protective materials.

How much danger asbestos poses for the ordinary citizen is a matter of controversy. Some people believe that there's too much asbestos around us and that it's a health hazard to everyone. This could be especially true for children and office workers, who spend much of their time indoors, often in buildings that use a good deal of asbestos for insulation. The U.S. government has been trying to have asbestos removed from the walls and ducts in such buildings. It is, however, a costly job: the EPA estimates that we have about 733,000 buildings with asbestos in them and that it will cost around $150 billion to get rid of it.[2]

Other people feel there is no cause for alarm, since the amounts that most people are exposed to are small, the regulations are strong enough to prevent problems, and the form of asbestos used in buildings is not as dangerous as other kinds.

It is better to be safe than sorry, however. Most of us can try to stay away from places where we know asbestos is widely used. We can use asbestos-free products and wear filtering masks when working with asbestos in insulating projects around the home. Above all, people who smoke should avoid doing so in offices or school buildings with asbestos walls and ceilings because one's chances of getting cancer are greater if one smokes and is exposed to asbestos, since both damage the lungs.

CARBON MONOXIDE

A very toxic colorless and odorless gas, carbon monoxide is present in the exhaust gases of cars and trucks. It should not be confused with carbon *dio*xide, also a colorless and odorless gas, which is found in the atmosphere or is formed when any fuel containing carbon is burned. Carbon dioxide is used to make soda water and other carbonated beverages and is also what we exhale during our normal breathing.

Carbon *mono*xide is not something one likes to associate with breathing. When it is inhaled, it combines with the hemoglobin in the blood — the substance in our red cells that carries oxygen — depriving a person of oxygen. In large doses it can easily kill. With so many cars and trucks on our highways, people everywhere are exposed to unhealthy concentrations of carbon monoxide.

CHLORINE

A poisonous, greenish yellow gas with a very bad, irritating smell when it is circulating by itself, chlorine is usually found with sodium in a more acceptable state as sodium chloride, or table salt. (A chloride is a compound of chlorine with another element.) Along with its partners, chlorine has many uses, most of them beneficial. It kills bacteria in drinking water, swimming pools, and sewage; in carbon tetrachloride, it cleans the spots out of our clothes and puts out fires; it bleaches laundry and paper; and it kills insects when it is in DDT and another powerful pesticide, chlordane.

Chlorine is important to environmentalists because it is a component of some of the other pollutants you'll encounter in this list and elsewhere in this book — CFCs, DDT, dioxin, PCBs, and vinyl chloride.

CHLOROFLUOROCARBONS (CFCs)

Chlorofluorocarbons are gassy mixtures of chlorine, fluorine (a poisonous gas), carbon (a common element found in all plants and animals), and sometimes hydrogen (the most abundant of the elements, it forms water when combined with oxygen).

CFCs are common industrial chemicals used in aerosols (spray cans), refrigerants, air conditioners, solvents (liquids that dissolve other substances), fire extinguishers, and in the manufacture of plastics. Scientists believe that as CFCs are poured into the atmosphere they destroy ozone, a form of oxygen that forms a layer in the earth's atmosphere and protects us from harmful ultraviolet rays. It is feared that the destruction of the ozone layer will bring harm to life on earth and cause disastrous climate changes.

DDT

This pesticide was widely used in the 1940s and 1950s and is perhaps the most familiar of the products that contain chlorine in one form or another. DDT is a blessedly shortened version of the pesticide's real chemical name, dichlorodiphenyltrichloroethane.

When he discovered the value of DDT as an insecticide in 1939, the Swiss chemist Paul Müller was highly praised — indeed, he won a Nobel Prize for the achievement in 1948. DDT became the first effective chemical weapon against insects. Little did Müller know how the tide of opinion would change a few decades later.

True, DDT is fast acting, relatively cheap, and long lasting. But that last advantage is also a major drawback. In the 1950s, many scientists started worrying about the way DDT refused to disappear once it was applied. There was also increasing evidence that the pesticide was killing more than just insects. DDT in a body of water, for example, was absorbed by microscopic plants and animals, and when those microorganisms were eaten by fish, the fish, which eat a lot of tiny organisms, accumulated more DDT in their bodies and died. Diving birds ate the fish, absorbed the DDT from them, and in turn died. The same thing seemed to be going on in a wide range of wildlife. A robin would eat a DDT-tainted worm and die. Animals that ate leaves coated with DDT also died.

DDT's persistence and lethal effects on wildlife have led the U.S. and some forty other countries to ban its use. However, millions of tons of it are still widely used in many parts of the world, including the developing countries, to wipe out the mosquitoes that cause malaria. As a result, we in the United States, along with people in other countries that have banned it, still get sprinkled with it as the pesticide, which persists in the atmosphere, blows over us on the winds and falls to the earth in snow and rain.

Despite its known hazards, it's easy to understand why DDT is still being used in some countries. More than 2.1 billion people are at risk of getting malaria because they live in areas where the disease is most common, and some 270 million people are already infected. Between one and two million people die of the tropical disease each year.

DDT does stop the mosquito that carries the microscopic parasite that causes malaria — but only for a while. The difficulty is that mosquitoes breed so fast that they quickly develop resistance to the pesticide, no matter how many tons of it are sprayed. When DDT was used in India in the 1950s, the number of malaria cases dropped dramatically from 75 million to 50,000, but by the late 1970s, the number of cases was back up again, to 6.5 million. Not so hard to imagine when you consider that a single female mosquito that is resistant to DDT could have 20 million offspring in just two months.[3] And while the mosquitoes are building up their resistance to DDT, the environment is being dangerously coated with it. According to one report, samples of bottled milk collected recently in India contained nearly ten times the amount of DDT allowed. The total amount of DDT that Indians take into their bodies each day is high enough to cause potential damage to the heart, liver, and brain.[4]

Again, a trade-off question is required. When such devastating tropical diseases as malaria exist, isn't it wiser to use a pesticide such as DDT and not worry so much about the environment? For many of the officials who must make such decisions in the affected parts of the world, the question of using DDT or not is not a choice between a right and a wrong, but a choice between two rights.

DIOXIN

There is no single chemical with the name dioxin. It is, rather, a family of nearly one hundred compounds that are formed during the manufacture of certain pesticides and herbicides (including Agent Orange, as we discussed earlier) and when paper is bleached to rid it of impurities and make it whiter. Some forms of dioxin are more dangerous than others, but the family of dioxin compounds is often referred to as the most toxic group of chemicals known. Some of the fears are well founded: just a pinpoint amount of one form is enough to kill a whole batch of laboratory guinea pigs.

How much, if any, health damage dioxin causes in humans is still unknown, and many scientists are examining the potential dangers. Some scientists feel the danger has been exaggerated and blame the media, Vietnam veterans, and politicians for the furor. They argue that dioxin's effects in animals do not necessarily occur in people and that the chemical may change when it's in the soil. They point out that the only illness that dioxin is known to cause in humans is a skin disease and that even in the most serious incident involving the release of dioxin — at Seveso, Italy, in the 1970s — nobody was killed or suffered long-term injuries. Others believe flat out that dioxin causes cancer and other diseases, as well as stillbirths.

Whatever the effects of dioxin, the fact remains that it is toxic and we are exposed to it. According to the U.S. Food and Drug Administration (FDA), a major food source of dioxin for Americans is bottom fish from the Great Lakes, an area of the country with a good deal of industrial activity and chemical production. Several years ago, states in the region discovered they had a dioxin problem and asked the FDA whether they should restrict fishing and advise people about which fish would be dangerous to eat. A scientist at the FDA addressed the concerns this way:

> Our advice was that, for a fishery whose fish average less than 25 parts per trillion of dioxin, you probably don't need to control consumption. But if the fish average more than 50 parts per trillion, you probably shouldn't eat them. Between those levels, consumption should be restricted — probably once a

week for the seasonal folks and no more than twice a month for people eating fish there year-round.[5]

Even though there is no definitive word on the health effects of dioxin, the chemical continues to pop in and out of the news these days, sometimes with scary headlines. Often, the stories are centered around attempts to get rid of waste dioxin. As in the Alar story, people are lined up on opposite sides. The EPA and other government agencies feel that the best way to deal with waste dioxin from pesticide plants is to burn it. Environmentalists feel that to incinerate dioxin is only to change one form of toxic chemical into another — that is, when it is burned, it emits fumes that are just as bad as the intact chemical.

People who live near incinerators are understandably fearful. But should their fears be allowed to block a disposal plan that scientists feel is acceptable? Do you think that scientists should give in because there is a loud outcry from the public? Should the government finance a health study in every community that has a chemical factory, a waste dump, or an incinerator? Is it enough to say, "Thou shalt not"?

These questions apply not just to dioxin but to all the chemicals on our list and to many of the other environmental threats that we face.

LEAD

Lead is a metal that has been around at least since the time of the ancient Romans, who associated it with the slow-moving planet Saturn. A soft, bluish white element, it makes a neat streak when you pull a bit of it across a sheet of paper, which is why it was once used in pencils. Today, the "lead" in pencils is graphite, a form of carbon. But lead itself can still be found in an enormous number of items. Lead is in paints and batteries, in water pipes and in the solder that joins cans, in bullets and in the shields that protect nuclear reactors, and in some gasolines. Other forms of lead are used in pesticides, in dyes, and in medicines.

Lead is very poisonous if it gets inside humans, either through contaminated water or when it is incinerated and its fumes are inhaled. It affects the nervous system, causing brain damage, lack of coordination, and hearing difficulties. Lead is especially harmful to children because their nervous systems are not fully developed and because their small bodies absorb more lead than an adult's. Many children have become ill by chewing on windowsills or furniture that has been coated with paint containing lead or by drinking water that has passed through pipes made of the metal. When lead is incinerated, it is especially dangerous because the particles that come from the furnace stacks are so fine they stick in the lungs and then find their way into the bloodstream and bone marrow. Lead is also found in incinerator ash, and when the ash is dumped, it can poison the soil and, thus, underground drinking water supplies.

Vast quantities of lead are also deposited on towns that are near lead and zinc smelters and mines. One lead-tainted place that has been in the news is Silver Valley in Idaho. The area is rich in minerals, and mining has been underway there for more than a hundred years. Over the last twenty years, however, lead pollution has given the region the reputation of being one of the worst of the nation's contaminated sites. The lead just poured down on the valley from the smelters and ran through the waterways. In one year alone, thirty tons of lead per square mile were dropped on the towns beneath the smelter, and nearly 200 children were poisoned. One woman, who lived in the area as a child, recalled, "My dad wouldn't even let me blow bubble gum because you'd get lead inside you just by opening your mouth."[6]

MERCURY

Mercury is a heavy element also known as quicksilver because it is the only metallic element that is a fluid at ordinary temperatures. You've probably seen it in some thermometers, and if you've ever tried to grab a drop or two of it when it's loose, you understand why it's called quicksilver.

Besides giving us a temperature reading in thermometers, mercury is also used in barometers and other scientific apparatus, in dental fillings and, in various forms, in eye ointments and as an antiseptic in the red dye called Mercurochrome. The silvery metal is also added to some latex paints to prevent bacteria and mildew from thriving.

Like most chemicals that have so many uses, mercury is potentially dangerous. Some years ago, it was widely used in various cosmetics but was eventually banned for such products because it has a tendency to build up in the body. Various studies had also shown that mercury caused tumors in mice and neurological damage in humans.

The public was first alerted to the dangers of mercury in the 1950s and 1960s when several hundred fishermen and residents of the village of Minamata in southern Japan became ill and died after eating fish contaminated with high levels of mercury. The mercury had gotten into the water when the village's largest company, a chemical plant, dumped waste in Minamata Bay. Minamata disease, as the illness was called by the townspeople, caused people to lose control of their legs and hands. Some women gave birth to deformed children, and a few of the children were born without brains.

Ever since the disaster, hundreds of people have gone to court seeking damages. The company paid out many millions to the victims and in cleanup costs, and two of its former executives received prison sentences. But cases are still before the courts, and no one knows when the story of Minamata disease will be finished.[7]

In 1969, the FDA set limits for mercury in foods. There is definitely a need for such regulations. In 1986, for example, the FDA checked 127 swordfish shipments from fifteen countries for mercury — and samples from more than 70 percent of the countries had illegal levels! Today, swordfish imported into this country are automatically held up until tests show that they meet the FDA's requirements.[8]

NITROGEN DIOXIDE

Nitrogen dioxide is another gaseous pollutant that comes from a car's exhaust pipe. When we inhale too much of it, it can irritate the lungs, cause pneumonia and bronchitis, and increase the risk of viral infection. Like so many chemical products that have harmful effects, nitrogen dioxide is derived from a very beneficial element, nitrogen, the gas that forms four-fifths of the atmosphere and is essential to all animals and plants.

NITROGEN FERTILIZERS

Plants need nitrogen to produce protein. When there is too little nitrogen in the soil, plants do not grow tall, their leaves lack a healthy green color, and they produce fewer fruits and vegetables. When fertilizer containing nitrogen is applied to the ground, the element changes into nitrate. When it rains, the nitrate seeps through the soil and gets into the groundwater supplies. High levels of nitrate in drinking water can cause illness and possibly birth defects.

Although legal limits have been set on how much nitrate can be present in drinking water, many water supplies throughout the world still contain far more nitrate than they should.

OZONE

While ozone is the gas that protects us from the sun's dangerous ultraviolet rays, it is also a pollutant when it is formed on earth. Ozone can be made commercially for use as a bleach, a water purifier, and an air freshener. It is also created from automobile exhaust. This occurs when energy from the sun causes hydrocarbons — which are produced by many engines and industrial processes — to react with the nitrogen oxides from cars and power plants. Ozone created from this process is a chief ingredient in urban smog, which is a combination of smoke, chemical pollutants, and fog in the air. Ground-level ozone can increase dangerously during hot and very sunny periods.

Ozone can damage crops and plants and may have serious health effects, including breathing difficulties and lung damage; it can also worsen asthma and heart disease.

PCBs

The initials stand for polychlorinated biphenyls. These are highly toxic industrial chemicals that first came into use in 1929, and there are more than a hundred different kinds. They have been used to insulate heavy electrical transformers in power plants, to receive and store electricity in many household appliances, and to give flexibility to paints and adhesives. PCBs are discharged into the air from factory smokestacks and when plastic wastes are burned.

PCBs can be stored in body fat and are believed to cause cancer. They have also been blamed for threatening many species, including the bald eagle, with extinction. For these reasons, PCBs are no longer manufactured. But because they were used for so long and because they do not break down easily, millions of pounds of the chemicals are still lying around in landfills and in our water supplies. In 1990, for instance, residents of a flooded area in Indiana were not allowed to return to their homes to pick up personal items because double the acceptable level of PCBs was detected in the area. Also, PCBs manage to remain in the atmosphere for years and continue to rain down on earth from time to time. It has been estimated that it will take twenty years to rid the earth of all the PCBs that have accumulated.

Once PCBs find their way into our food sources, they cannot be eliminated. According to the FDA, PCBs are most noticeable in freshwater fish, especially the coho and chinook salmon from the Great Lakes and bottom-feeding freshwater species from waters near other industrial areas. Coastal fish may also contain PCBs. The FDA's regulations require that any food with more than the tolerance level be seized.

POLYMERS

There are natural polymers and synthetic ones. The natural ones include proteins and starches. The synthetic ones are the components of plastics and many man-made fabrics, including some familiar names: nylon, Teflon, Styrofoam, polyester, and spandex, to name but a few. Polymers can cause many environmental problems. When they are burned, they throw deadly pollutants into the air; when some of them are buried in dumps, toxic substances they contain may seep out into the groundwater; when plastics are being manufactured, chemicals in them may be inhaled by the workers and cause severe reactions.

SODIUM NITRITE

A salt used to preserve cured foods such as bacon, bologna, and various smoked hams and fish, sodium nitrite combines with natural stomach chemicals to form nitrosamines. These are among the most potent cancer-causing compounds known and are still being intensely studied. Some food processors are using substitutes for sodium nitrite or have reduced the amount they put in food. Cigarette smoke also contains many powerful nitrosamines.

SULFUR DIOXIDE

A heavy gas with a sharp odor, sulfur dioxide occurs in nature during volcanic activity and when organic material decays. It is also formed when sulfur, coal, oil, or natural gas is burned. When sulfur dioxide and nitrogen dioxide are discharged into the air, they contribute to acid rain, which can kill plants and cause other ecological damage.

VINYL CHLORIDE

Vinyl chloride is a gaseous compound that is used to make polyvinyl chloride (PVC), the most widely used of the vinyl plastics. It is toxic when inhaled.

SOME SOLUTIONS

Do we really need all these chemicals? If you consider this question carefully, chances are you'll conclude that indeed we need some of them. Banning all chemicals would be as silly as banning the use of electricity because it can electrocute people, or banning butter because it contains cholesterol, which can harden our arteries. I doubt that any of us wants to go back to the Stone Age. Again, chemicals are important to just about every aspect of our lives. They keep us healthy and feed and clothe us. Given that, you have to weigh the benefits against the risks when considering what to do about the chemical barrage that seems to be directed against us.

The only solution to the chemical assault on the environment is to take more responsibility for it. The chemical industry must show responsibility by carefully testing the chemicals they produce before they release them, by being careful about which chemical products they produce, how they produce them, and how they transport them, and by seeing that the waste products that are created in manufacturing these chemicals are disposed of safely. The people who use the chemicals have a responsibility, too. They must use them with discretion and perhaps even refuse to use certain ones. And the users, too, must learn how to clean up after themselves.

This advice from Dr. Jenny Pronczuk deGarbino, a toxicologist at Universidad de la República in Uruguay, should be heeded:

> Scientific progress is certainly a need in such areas as medicine, food technology, agriculture, and energy. But do we really need such an array of household products just to keep our homes clean and fragrant? Do we really need hundreds of variegated cosmetics in order to look good?
>
> The more chemicals we have around us, the higher the risks of falling victim to them. We have to consider all the social, cultural, and educational factors related to each episode of poisoning. A molecule by itself, a drug in a flask, or a pesticide in a tank may be totally innocent. The risk starts when too many molecules appear, when too many drugs are being used or

when tons of pesticides are applied indiscriminately. Poison-
ings result from a surplus of chemicals in our society, coupled
with a lack of information, respect and discretion in their
use.[9]

2
THE PROBLEM:

TOO MUCH NOISE

Not too long ago, a skyscraper in Manhattan was actually fined for making too much noise. The seventy-two-story building is topped by a ribbed, eight-sided dome 800 feet above the ground, and wind blowing over it was apparently generating a high-pitched whistle that drew hundreds of complaints from neighbors, some of them many blocks away. As one nearby resident put it, "You think you're in a loony bin. You can't get away from it."[1]

A whistling building, while not that common, is one more example of a form of pollution — noise — that is all too often ignored when assaults on the environment are discussed. Noise, like offensive odors, is classified as a sensory pollutant, one that affects our senses. In the case of noise, it is our hearing and our ability to think clearly that are impaired.

The dictionary offers a number of definitions of noise:

Loud, confused, or senseless shouting or outcry.
A sound that lacks agreeable musical quality or is noticeably unpleasant.
Any sound that is undesired or interferes with one's hearing of something.

An unwanted signal or disturbance in an electronic communication system (such as radio or television).

Scientifically, noise is defined a bit more precisely. It is measured on what scientists call a decibel scale. Decibels are the units used to compare the intensity of sounds. For example, a whisper or the ticking of a watch measures about 20 decibels, a suburban street without traffic about 40, ordinary conversation about 60 decibels, a noisy restaurant 70, city traffic about 90, a typical rock concert or a hammer banging on a steel plate about 110, a jet engine from one hundred feet away about 130.

Loud noise is classified as a pollutant because it is not only annoying but also harmful to our physical and psychological health. Sound is actually a series of mechanical vibrations traveling through the air. These vibrations create pressure in our ears, and if the pressure is great enough or is experienced for a prolonged period of time, the sensitive, innermost portions of the ears can be damaged. In general, prolonged exposure to any sound at or above ninety decibels — especially if the sound is high-pitched — can cause partial to severe hearing loss. (Sounds around 120 decibels can be very painful, and a sound that loud can probably damage one's hearing permanently.)[2]

There are many occupations, from rock musician to construction worker, that expose people to the damaging effects of long periods of loud noise. Farmers who work with tractors and other machinery are especially prone to trouble: half of older farmers and a quarter of younger ones experience hearing loss. Many workers wear ear protectors. In addition, there are laws that govern the number of hours a worker may be exposed to loud noise per day. For instance, a worker exposed to ninety decibels of noise should not work in such an environment for more than eight hours; someone should not be exposed to one hundred decibels, about what you get at a rock concert, for more than two hours.

Of course, it is not only workers on noisy jobs who are at risk. Every day, every one of us can be annoyed, and perhaps injured, by noise pollution. Passenger jets roar overhead, creating a din that is even worse for those who live near airports. Indeed, the United States' commercial air fleet numbers about 4,800 airliners, and around 2,350 of those are of the noisier variety.[3] Car and motorcycle engines are revved up regularly in neighborhoods all over the world, stereos and television sets blare, garbage trucks create deafening noises on every city street, horns honk, trains rumble by, air conditioners whine, road construction crews shatter the air with their backhoes and jackhammers, loudspeakers shout political slogans. One Japanese study tells us that because noise and vibrations of all kinds are so prevalent in our daily lives, they account for 40 percent of pollution-related complaints in Japan.[4]

SOME SOLUTIONS

Tough laws can help. Many communities have departments of environmental protection whose responsibility is to check out harsh noise in everything from discos to factories to air-conditioning units. Inspectors have the authority to charge offenders who violate so-called noise control codes. Roads can be improved so that vehicle tires do not create as much noise, traffic control can be more strictly enforced, factories can install quieter machinery and better insulation. In the case of the airlines, the U.S. Congress and the Administration recently agreed on measures that would eliminate most of the noisier jets from our skies by the end of the 1990s; the noisy planes will be replaced by new, quieter jets. Scientists, of course, are learning more about how sound behaves and are working hard to come up with other ways to insulate us from unwanted sound.

In general, though, preventing noise pollution is a matter of consideration: everyone has to think of others before turning up the stereo full volume, using a vacuum cleaner or a lawn mower when others are trying to sleep, or blasting off on a motorcycle on a quiet street.

3
THE PROBLEM:

BAD AIR

> Smoke lowering down from chimney pots, making a soft black drizzle, with flakes of soot in it as big as full-grown snowflakes — gone into mourning, one might imagine, for the death of the sun. . . . Fog everywhere . . . fog down the river, where it rolls defiled among the tiers of shipping, and the waterside pollutions of a great (and dirty) city.
>
> — Charles Dickens, *Bleak House*

That dingy scene is not just a fictional picture from England's industrial past. It may be seen today almost everywhere on earth. Great clouds of yellowish smog and black smoke hang over the world's factory cities and waft across borders to cloud the skies over rural areas, regions that were once spared such an intrusion. It is not only smokestacks that blot out the sun and pollute the air. Automobiles and trucks spew fumes skyward. Fireplaces and home furnaces, burning leaves in the fall, barbecue grills in the summertime — all contribute to dirtying the air. Indoors, things are not much brighter. From rooms full of cigarette smoke to the Third World's overcrowded mud-and-thatch huts choked with the smoke from wood and coal fires, poor air quality is affecting the health of millions of people. And along with the smoke, there is acid rain, a noxious chemical drizzle loaded with industrial emissions that fall from the skies to pollute rivers, streams, lakes, fertile farmlands, and forests and corrode some of the world's ancient, historic monuments. If Dickens were alive today, he would not be surprised at all.

Air pollution is among our most serious environmental concerns. One of the worst cases of it was, of course, the Bhopal disaster in India, in which a cloud of poisonous gas released by the Union Carbide chemical company killed more than 3,000 people and severely injured hundreds of thousands more. Not all cases of air pollution are so horrid, but they are bad enough. And unless stronger steps are taken to curb air pollution, it will worsen, and so, too, will its effects on our health, our natural resources, and our food crops. Consider the following:

> • Between 1900 and 1985, the world's annual emission of sulfur dioxide increased sixfold, while nitrogen oxide emissions increased ten times over. These gases, along with the hydrocarbons that also result from the burning of fossil fuels by power plants and motor vehicles, are the chief sources of both urban air pollution and of the acid rain that sprinkles down just about everywhere.[1] In 1986 alone, more than six million tons of hydrocarbons and eight million tons of nitrogen oxide were put into the air by motor vehicles in the U.S.

> • The number of cars in the world is expected to grow from 400 million today to 700 million over the next twenty years. Much of that growth will occur in the developing world, which currently owns only 12 percent of the world's car fleet.[2]

> • In the U.S., air pollution causes as many as 120,000 deaths a year and costs some $40 billion a year in health care and lost work time.[3] Roughly 120 million Americans live in areas whose air is considered unhealthy by the Environmental Protection Agency.

> • In 1988, nearly 20,000 U.S. industrial plants put 2.4 billion pounds of toxic chemicals into the air.

• In the Czechoslovakian town of Bratislava, cancers have risen by a third, heart complaints by 40 percent, infant mortality by two-thirds and miscarriages by half since 1970, thanks to deadly air pollutants from nearby industries.[4]

• Three billion pounds of pesticides are sprayed on fields all over the world each year, and when it vaporizes, much of it travels up into the atmosphere.

• In Athens, Greece, the number of deaths rises sixfold on heavily polluted days. In Hungary, every twenty-fourth disability and every seventeenth death is caused by air pollution. In Bombay, India, breathing the air is the same as smoking ten cigarettes a day. And in Mexico, the capital has been declared a hardship post for diplomats because of the unhealthy air.[5]

• More than three million American youths under eighteen years of age smoke 947 million packs of cigarettes every year. Of the 2.3 billion people who are today under twenty years old, about 800 million are expected to become smokers, and if current smoking patterns continue, approximately 250 million of them will die from diseases induced by this form of air pollution.[6] And it is not only smokers who suffer. According to the World Health Organization, researchers have found that children living with smokers are much more often admitted to hospitals for upper respiratory conditions than children from nonsmoking families.

• Between 400 and 500 million people suffer from severe indoor air pollution as a direct result of fuels burned in the hearth.[7]

In Charles Dickens's time, the main source of air pollution was coal burning. Coal is dirty, and when it burns, it throws off toxic gases unless scrubbers — devices that weaken gases — are used. However, coal is still burned today in many countries where it is plentiful and cheap. Indeed, in the United States — where about 30 percent of the world's known coal reserves are — coal is the largest natural energy resource. If all the coal-fired utilities were closed down, the lights would be turned out in more than half the homes in America.

Coal is still a serious air polluter in places such as eastern Europe,

India, and China, where forms that contain a lot of sulfur are burned routinely and often without the advanced technology that can make them relatively clean. In India, for example, sulfur dioxide emissions from coal and oil nearly tripled between the early sixties and the late seventies.[8] Even the U.S., with all of its technical ability to make coal clean, has its share of coal-polluting troubles: a recent study by the National Research Council concluded that sulfur dioxide emissions from a coal-fired power plant near the Grand Canyon were contributing significantly to the smoky air over the canyon much of the year. The plant, which burns 24,000 tons of coal a day and releases twelve to thirteen tons of sulfur dioxide every hour, has no scrubbers.[9] Coal's use is also expanding. China, in fact, plans to double its use of coal by the end of this century, and it is expected that the developing countries will increase their use of coal by some 150 percent by the year 2005.

In many parts of the world, the U.S. among them, automobiles and industries are now the chief cause of air pollution. Here, while new fuel-efficient automobiles are sending far fewer hydrocarbons into the air than ever before, there are some 72 million more vehicles on the nation's highways — which means that cars still emit around 45 percent of all manufactured hydrocarbons. Industries have also cut back the number of pollutants they discharge into the air, but industry has grown, too, and has added to the air pollution problem by its use of tall smokestacks that spread pollutants over wide areas.[10] In one especially bad attack of chlorine smog pouring from five chemical facilities in the Soviet Union recently, children fainted during school assemblies and other people with breathing difficulties flocked to hospitals. "People are Perishing Without a War," said the headline in one local newspaper. "Enough!"[11] In 1989, vacant lots where chromium — a metal often used to make other metals shiny — had been buried were giving off chromium dust, which turned up in dangerously high levels in the air ducts of an elementary school in Jersey City, New Jersey; elevated levels of the airborne pollutant turned up in the urine of many of the schoolchildren who were tested after the school was ordered closed.[12]

Another cause of air pollution is what scientists call biomass burning. You could call it lighting a bonfire. Biomass burning, which goes on all over the world, is the intentional lighting of fires to burn off forests and shrubbery to make room for development, agriculture, and grazing, to clear away agricultural waste, or, in the case of burning wood and dung, to provide fuel and heat. According to scientists, fires cover 2 to 5 percent of the earth's surface every year, and humans light more than 95 percent of them.[13] What's the matter with bonfires? Well, scientists now know that biomass burning releases hundreds of substances, many of them toxic, including hydrocarbons, which, as we've discussed, can form acid rain. Moreover, when the hydrocarbons and other chemicals mix with sunlight, they form ozone, the noxious gas we discussed earlier that protects us from the sun's rays but that also can contribute to lung disease when we inhale it and can damage plants.

When biomass burning is done indoors for cooking and heating without proper ventilation, as it is in rural Africa and Asia by millions of people, the results can be lethal. In Africa, the typical home-fire scene involves a fire inside the house with a cooking pot resting on three stones. The fuel is usually agricultural waste, logs, branches, leaves, or dried dung from animals. Burning this material inside a small, sometimes windowless hut creates large quantities of choking smoke and irritating gases. Studies carried out by the World Health Organization in African houses have measured levels of dangerous chemicals high enough to be a definite health hazard. Indeed, wood smoke was shown in the studies to cause breathing problems in young children, and babies were being born seriously underweight when their mothers were exposed to such air pollution.

Unfortunately, we often tend to forget this form of air pollution because we are so concerned about what comes out of the smokestacks and tail pipes of our more developed cities. But, as the World Health Organization points out:

> Village dust and the smoke of cooking fires serve as a constant eye irritant. Chronic lung diseases, including tuberculosis, habitually besiege rural populations of the Third World, adding yet another burden to the impossible survival course of everyday existence. Exposure to biomass fuel emissions in

developing countries is probably the single most important occupational health hazard to women.[14]

We've mentioned acid rain as a product of air pollution, and it is a dangerous one. Acid rain, full of hydrocarbons and other gaseous pollutants such as sulfur dioxide and nitrogen oxide, sours our soil, forests, and water. Fortunately, acid rain is not yet a crisis, but it is bad enough. A ten-year study ordered by Congress in 1980 recently came up with the following conclusions that confirmed many scientists' fears:

• Aquatic life in about 10 percent of eastern lakes and streams is being damaged by acid rain, much of the damage occurring when snow melts in the spring, sending acidic water into streams.

• Stone and metal structures are being corroded by acid rain.

• Red spruce trees are finding it difficult to withstand the stress of cold temperatures because of the toxic rain.

• While the majority of North American forests are healthy, the buildup of acid rain might lead to a decline in forests over the next decades.[15]

All the forms of air pollution we have mentioned injure the air that we breathe. There is another form of pollution that passes through the air but causes problems far higher up, in the upper atmosphere. This kind of pollution is caused by the discharge of chemicals that damage the earth's ozone layer. We mentioned that ozone is itself a pollutant, the chief ingredient of urban smog. It contaminates the air around us and ruins our crops and trees after it is formed from the gases that belch from car tail pipes. In its natural state, however, high in the upper atmosphere, it is a protector — it prevents the sun's life-threatening ultraviolet radiation from reaching us.

The faraway ozone that shields us is in an invisible layer, twenty-five miles overhead, that is formed when ultraviolet radiation reacts with oxygen. But for all its power in filtering out the sun's heavy-duty rays — rays that cause not only sunburn but eye disorders, weakened bodily defenses against diseases, and cancer — the ozone shield is a fragile piece of work. It can be damaged and worn away easily, and one way this occurs is when we pour chlorofluorocarbons (CFCs) into the air. CFCs are compounds that are released from spray cans, refrigeration systems, and blown-foam materials, and when they get up into the ozone layer, they are broken up by the fierce ultraviolet radiation. When that happens, chlorine is released — a single atom of which can destroy 100,000 molecules of ozone.

We have been releasing CFCs into the atmosphere for many years, and though scientists speculated that the chemicals were damaging the ozone shield, it was not until 1985 that researchers had definite proof: they found a hole in the ozone layer over Antarctica; it had formed because the intense cold above the frozen continent boosted the chlorine's power to react with ozone. Since then, ozone depletion has occurred fairly regularly over Antarctica. It is estimated that over the years, as much as half the Antarctican ozone layer has been destroyed, with the loss of more than 95 percent at some altitudes.[16] So much CFC remains in the atmosphere that scientists fear ozone depletion will continue well into the next century, and not only over Antarctica but elsewhere in the upper atmosphere. Indeed, ozone holes have also been reported over the North Pole, and according to some reports, the ozone screen has thinned about 5 percent from Oslo, Norway, to New Orleans during the past ten years.[17] Moreover, air that has been stripped of its ozone may be carried to other regions of the world, where it could possibly dilute other concentrations of ozone.

SOME SOLUTIONS

Dealing with the sources of air pollution, as with all the other forms of pollution, is not always easy. Some people argue, for example, that the acid rain issue has been blown out of proportion and that there is no need to spend a lot of money on expensive control measures. Some power plant operators do not want to pay for costly scrubbers in their coal-fired plants unless they are ordered to do so. And switching to less polluting means of generating energy — such as shifting from the use of fossil fuels, which currently supply 75 percent of the world's energy needs, to solar and wind power and other alternatives — is viewed by many people as much too unrealistic.

There are a few bright spots. Air pollution levels have declined over the last ten years. According to the EPA's inventory of toxic substances released by industries into the environment, 4.5 billion pounds of poisonous chemicals went into the nation's land, air, and water in 1988 — an enormous amount, but nine percent less than what was discharged in 1987.[18] New cars emit 96 percent fewer hydrocarbons per mile than they did in 1970, and smokestack scrubbers and the use of low sulfur fuels in power plants have cut sulfur dioxide emissions by as much as 25 percent. American industry and consumers now spend some $35 billion a year to control air pollution, and the effort has reduced lead concentrations by 90 percent, sulfur dioxide by 35 percent, carbon monoxide by 32 percent, nitrogen oxides by 12 percent, and ozone by 16 percent. If measures had not been taken, some U.S. cities would be as bad off as Mexico City, which ranks among the worst urban environments.[19]

There is also a new Clean Air Act, which strengthens the laws aimed at reducing air pollution. The new act contains numerous requirements, including the following:

• A reduction by one-half of the amounts of sulfur dioxide and nitrogen oxide, the pollutants most responsible for acid rain formation, that may be released from industrial smokestacks each year.

• The listing of 189 toxic chemicals — in the past, only seven were regulated.

• Phasing out the production of chlorofluorocarbons (CFCs), the chemicals that destroy the earth's ozone shield, with a total ban by the year 2000.

• Stricter tail-pipe emission standards for cars; beginning in 1998, all new automobiles must have pollution control equipment that will last for ten years or 100,000 miles.

Whether the new law will make a big difference in air pollution and in protecting the fragile ozone shield remains to be seen. But it is, at least, a positive sign.

In the meantime, we can all help in small ways — by not smoking, perhaps driving less, maybe even using the outdoor barbecue less often.

4
THE PROBLEM:

DYING WATER

When acid rain falls from the sky, when oil spills from a damaged tanker or during offshore drilling for oil, when toxic chemicals are discharged into the water by factories and farms, when sewage sludge is poured into harbors, water is damaged. When the pollution is so extensive that wildlife is unable to live in or near a body of water, the water itself is considered dead. Even without pollution, water is in constant danger of dying — it can dry up as a result of drought, overirrigation, or just plain wastefulness.

Most times it is very easy to tell when water supplies have dwindled or died because of overuse. Dry streambeds and riverbeds, low levels in reservoirs and lakes, and parched farmlands are all evidence of scarce water. Death of a body of water by pollution may also be easy to see. The beautiful blue Danube, immortalized in a famous waltz, is one sad example. It sweeps majestically through central Europe from its source in the Black Forest of Germany, a sight to behold for much of the way. But as it winds the 2,000 miles toward the Black Sea, it picks up sewage and chemicals, waste that has been discharged into it and into its tributaries. Heavily weighted now by the refuse, its movement slows, and by the time the Danube empties into the sea it is full of scum, a sluggish, swollen mess that would hardly inspire the author of the "Blue Danube" waltz, Johann Strauss, were he alive today. The Vistula River in Poland, the country's watery industrial dump, also drags along, as slow as molasses — and the same color as that brownish syrup as well. In Venice, the once picturesque waterways where gondolas have long transported awed tourists are now clogged with stinking, yellowish brown slime, the result of tons of pollutants. Our own awesome Great Lakes, which hold a fifth of the world's fresh water, are full of smelly scum and foam in places, a witch's brew of toxic chemicals and floating oil. On the Chinese island of Taiwan, where a huge petrochemical industry flourishes, nearly every river has been so visibly polluted that scientists there often use the term *pronounced dead* when taking water samples.

Sometimes, a dying water supply is not so easy to diagnose. Your untrained eye would not be able to tell when a water table — the upper part of the ground that has been saturated with water — is dropping. Neither can you see the diminishing supply of water in aquifers, underground water sources formed when cracks or spaces in rock and earth fill with water. It also may be hard to tell that the water in the ocean or a lake is dying. The toxic chemicals that are killing it may not be visible for the moment, but they are taking their toll on the microscopic plants and animals that live beneath the surface by blocking the sunlight essential for their growth or by poisoning them outright.

But before we talk about how water dies and about some of the specific problems that affect different bodies of water, let's find out something about water, that colorless fluid we are all so familiar with. First of all, there's plenty of it: water covers about 74 percent of the earth's surface, and there are trillions and trillions of gallons of it. That we need it is obvious. We need water to help us digest our food, to bring nutrients to various organs, and to help us rid our bodies of wastes. We can survive for weeks without food but only a few days without water. If you've read Samuel Taylor Coleridge's "Rime of the Ancient Mariner," you might recall the lines that tell of the pain of great thirst:

And every tongue, through utter drought,
Was withered at the root;
We could not speak, no more than if
We had been choked with soot.

We use a lot of water in the United States, about 400 million gallons every day; 119 million gallons of that is for drinking. Half of the water we use comes from lakes, rivers, streams, and reservoirs, the rest from aquifers.

People are not, of course, the only ones who drink water. A cow has to drink three gallons of water to produce one gallon of milk, and a stalk of corn needs twenty-six gallons to grow tall.[1] Without water from vast irrigation systems, places such as California's Central Valley, where huge amounts of our fruits and vegetables are grown, would be lucky to grow just weeds. Water has many other jobs besides quenching our thirst and feeding crops. We use it for fun, to swim and boat in. We harvest food from it, such as fish and shellfish, even edible seaweed. Industry uses vast quantities of water to wash, cool, and manufacture materials. It takes an astonishing 1,400 gallons of water to produce everything that goes into one fast-food meal of a hamburger, French fries, and a soft drink. It takes 39,000 gallons to make a whole automobile and 70 gallons to produce a gallon of gasoline. We use water to transport many products on ships and barges.[2]

Water is also harnessed to generate electricity. The generation of electricity with water is called hydroelectric power, and it is the source of about a third of the world's electricity. Hydroelectric power employs water from a waterfall, tides, or fast-moving rivers to turn a turbine, which drives a generator. This form of power is cheap because water, the fuel, is free.

What is water? We all know what it looks and feels like, and that it falls from the clouds as rain and forms our streams and seas. It is also the main ingredient in all living things — bees and baboons, humans and hogs and hollyhocks. Three-quarters of the human body is composed of water, the same percentage that covers the earth. In fact, all life — all one million species of animals and 350,000 species of plants — began, it is believed, in the primitive earth's oceans.

Around a billion years after the earth was formed, very simple one-celled organisms appeared. These evolved into more elaborate life forms, insectlike creatures among them, which eventually came out of the sea and adapted to life on the land. Later, some fish also left the water and, again, through the process of adaptation, became comfortable living on the land as amphibians, reptiles, and finally mammals, the category that includes humans. Perhaps this history is why we carry so much water around in our bodies and need it to survive.

Water's unique chemistry makes it a conducive home for a variety of life-forms. Made up of hydrogen and oxygen, water combines readily with all kinds of substances essential to life; without water, many important chemical reactions could not take place in our bodies. But though water sustains life, it is not itself all that durable. Water can be damaged just as any chemical mixture can. In fact, every time we use water, we change its quality. When we dump toxic chemicals, sewage, oil, or any debris into it, we alter its delicate balance of chemicals and its biological and physical appearance. In effect, we kill it. The changes that occur when we spoil water are what we know as pollution — and pollution of water makes it unfit to drink, causes disease, ruins fishing and boating, and destroys aquatic plants and animals.

It is hard to imagine water dying, especially when we see stunning color photographs in travel brochures and nature magazines that display sparkling waterfalls, roaring, foam-churned rivers, placid green ponds, deep blue lakes, perhaps a crystal-clear stream bubbling along in the winter with fresh white snow heaped on both banks. The world still has such beautiful examples of water in nature and, it is hoped, will preserve them for many centuries.

But nature alone cannot keep our precious water cover both beautiful and useful. It is true that we'll always have new supplies of water as long as vapor continues to condense in the atmosphere and fresh water continues to seep into the ground and into the oceans. This process is all part of what we know as the ecological equilibrium, the way that nature maintains its balance. We know that nature manages to replenish what it loses — animals eat one another in just the right numbers to prevent one species from overrunning the earth, and so, too, do insects and fish. In other species, fast reproduction makes up for deaths, even when the death rate is enormously high because of some natural disaster.

Human beings, however, have a knack for upsetting the balance of nature. Yes, there are times when this must be done, as when insects that carry disease have to be eradicated with pesticides or when the growth of weeds threatens a food crop and has to be stopped with herbicides. But we have to be careful how much insecticide and herbicide, and what kind, we dust our earth with, and we need to be wary, too, of what and how much we put into the sky and the water. If the atmosphere keeps getting polluted with chemical smoke, what kind of rain will fall into the oceans? If we keep dumping toxic chemicals directly into the water, what kind of water will result?

Nature does have the capacity to deal effectively with such assaults on water, but nature can be overwhelmed when our polluting activities run out of control. In the case of the canals in Venice, scientists say that three times as much pollutant enters the water as the ecosystem can deal with, and that it may take ten years to reduce the pollutants to the equilibrium level.[3] It is like what happens when you put a drop of ink into a glass of water and stir it up. A drop or two won't be too noticeable, but as you put in more ink, the water starts to take on color. If you put in a lot of ink, the water will look like ink. Likewise, trace amounts of metals or toxic chemicals probably won't do too much damage to a large body of water, but tons of these substances will, especially when many different kinds of materials are mixed together.

Many of the pollutants we have already mentioned damage water. Dana Kester, a professor of oceanography at the University of Rhode Island, lists six major types of marine pollutants:

> • Metals such as copper, lead, cadmium, and mercury, which can be toxic to tiny marine organisms and humans. These metals are absorbed by organisms and eventually find their way into the sediments on the seafloor.

• Synthetic compounds that include PCBs, the pesticide DDT, and plastics. When they accumulate and interact with natural marine processes, they can disrupt the life cycles or metabolism of various organisms and when they get inside fish, can make them inedible.

• Petroleum hydrocarbons that leak or spill into the water and affect birds and sea life.

• Nitrates and phosphates released by farms and industries. While these substances may be made into beneficial fertilizers, they can also limit marine life. They do this by stimulating the explosive growth of decaying nuisance weeds, so-called algal blooms (*algal* refers to algae, a large group of mostly aquatic plants that includes some of the simplest organisms known). The growth of these blooms shifts the natural balance among species by robbing the water of oxygen; without oxygen, sea creatures suffocate and die. The algae also may produce poisons that can kill fish directly.

• Degradable organic material, such as sewage waste. As this stuff breaks down, it eats up dissolved oxygen in the water and thus competes with the plants and the animals that need the oxygen to "breathe."

• Viruses, bacteria, and parasites, which can cause disease and infections in humans.[4]

Besides dumped pollutants, irrigation systems — systems that supply water to farms — are also to blame for the poor quality of much of our water. Recently, a committee of experts from the National Research Council, which conducts various scientific studies that are in the public's interest, pointed out that agriculture in the western part of the United States has long been necessarily tied to irrigation. Indeed, irrigation today accounts for nearly 90 percent of the region's water usage; in California, 83 percent of water consumption is attributed to agriculture.[5]

While irrigation is essential, the difficulty, as the committee said, is that irrigation creates salinity, that is, salts dissolved in irrigation water become concentrated as the water evaporates under the hot western sun. When the concentration of these salts is high enough, they can be toxic to plants and other organisms. A third of all irrigated lands in the U.S. may suffer some damage from salinity, and the damage is costly: in the Colorado River basin alone, according to the committee, salinity problems have cost agriculture more than $100 million a year over the last decade.

But it is not only salt that is to blame. In 1982, after waterfowl started dying in California's Kesterson National Wildlife Refuge, attention was focused on an entirely new phenomenon, toxic levels of selenium, a naturally occurring trace element that is used to make various electronic components and to vulcanize rubber, that is, to make it more durable and more elastic. Apparently, the selenium had leached out from surrounding farmland and concentrated in the irrigation water. Other trace elements, including the deadly poison arsenic, have also turned up in other western sites. While the committee noted that the trace-element contamination did not pose a significant threat to human health, it warned that the potential for danger exists wherever sites show signs of such contamination or high levels of agricultural chemicals.[6]

Something you should know more about when the subject is water pollution is the food chain, for it is vital to the survival of all living things. When it is disrupted by pollution — on land or in the water — the consequences can be devastating to the environment. Essentially, the food chain is the process by which a larger organism consumes one smaller than itself for food or energy. The first link in the food chain is green plants. This category includes simple algae, which grow in the water, as well as more complex plants that are found on land, what we refer to as the higher plants. The green plants have to get their food and energy from somewhere, of course, and they find a plentiful source in sunlight. The process is a very complicated one, but in general, here is how plants acquire and use their food: There is a key element in plants called chlorophyll, and it is what makes them green. Chlorophyll is more than just a coloring agent, however. It also absorbs light and is able to convert it into chemical energy, which is then turned into carbohydrates, the sugars and starches that are a major class of animal foods. The process by which green plants get their food and energy from light is called photosynthesis, and it is easy to understand how this first link in the food chain can be disrupted when pollutants block out the sunlight.

After the plants, the next step up in the food chain is the herbivores, animals that eat plants. Next, the herbivores are eaten by carnivores, meat eaters, which may also themselves be eaten by other carnivores. (Unless you have a preference, eating only vegetables, you and a lot of other humans are generally omnivores, that is, you eat both vegetables and animals in maintaining your place in the food chain.) The last link in the food chain is made up of what have been called the demolishers and the reducers — bacteria and fungi, which live on and break down decaying animal and plant waste.

Among the most important living links in the water's food chain are microscopic animals and plants called plankton, which drift and float under the influence of ocean currents. The plant members of this group are called phytoplankton, and they are mainly algae found in the upper reaches of the sea, where friendly light can reach them. Sometimes there are so many of them that they color the water with a greenish bloom, and because of this they are often known as the grass of the sea. Plankton account for a third to a half of all the photosynthesis on the planet. Phytoplankton are eaten by tiny creatures called zooplankton, which may be the eggs, larvae (the immature forms of insects or of some animals), or adults of anything from one-celled animals to jellyfish. Zooplankton generally live deep in the water and are an important food for whales and a wide variety of fish.

But plankton are endangered. As more and more pollutants pour into the seas, plankton are deprived of their nourishing sunlight and of chemical nutrients in the water. Sea-grass beds may be destroyed outright, or, when certain algae members of the plankton family grow uncontrollably because of too many fertilizers dumped into the water, they are transformed into lethal blooms that kill other sea life rather than nourish them. The ozone hole we've talked about can also damage phytoplankton. Recently, scientists found that the increase in ultraviolet radiation caused by the ozone hole over the frozen continent of Antarctica can harm the production of phytoplankton by decreasing the rate of photosynthesis of the algal cells and destroying chlorophyll. One of the scientists who investigated the problem, Dr. Sayed Z. El-Sayed of Texas A & M University, concluded:

> Since the phytoplankton are the basic primary producers in the Antarctic Ocean on which all other components of the ecosystem (zooplankton, tiny planktonic creatures called krill, fish, squid, winged birds, seals and whales) depend for their livelihood, any substantial decrease in the productivity of these waters, or any change in their community structure, could have far-reaching ecological implications.[7]

Contamination of the marine environment, of course, does more than upset the food chain and cause the death of the fish and seabirds that make water their home. It affects us, too. When pollutants get into our water supply, the water that is so essential to our lives and well-being becomes undrinkable. In 1990, an underground storage tank near the Pawcatuck River in Stonington, Connecticut, leaked 1,500 gallons of gasoline and threatened the water supply for 31,000 people. Connecticut depends almost entirely on groundwater for drinking, and with more than 50,000 underground tanks — not including residential tanks and chemical tanks that are unregulated — containing gasoline and fuel oil, it is no wonder there is deep concern in the state. Many of the tanks need replacement and are likely to leak.[8]

Connecticut is not, of course, the only place that has drinking-water problems. Contamination is widespread and has, in fact, been with us for years. In 1908, 20,000 people in New York City became sick from cholera, a disease that causes severe diarrhea and abdominal pain and can kill. Typhoid fever, another waterborne disease, killed many people in the U.S. during the early 1900s until public health officials started treating water with chlorine, a chemical that disinfects both drinking water and the water in swimming pools. But while chlorine stopped cholera and typhoid, it didn't help when toxic chemicals started leaking into the water supply. Between 1969 and 1972, New Orleans's public water supply, which comes from the Mississippi River, was found to contain sixty-six different chemicals.[9]

Even the passage of the Safe Drinking Water Act by Congress in 1974 — which sets standards for water quality and regulates water treatment — has not stopped the pollution. Since the act's passage, more than 2,100 contaminants, including lead and even the by-products of the chlorine disinfecting treatment, have been found in one or more drinking-water systems. Nearly 200 of the contaminants, 100 of them cancer causing, are known or believed to have dangerous health effects at certain levels.[10]

Lead poisoning is one of the most serious illnesses linked to bad water. Even though the U.S. government has strict laws that limit the amount of lead in drinking water, many thousands of schoolchildren are still drinking water that is highly contaminated with the metal. In fact, the Environmental Protection Agency estimates that more than 250,000 children are exposed to lead in their drinking water each year — at levels high enough to affect their mental and physical development.[11]

Another dangerous pollutant in water is the various forms of nitrogen. Nitrogen is a colorless, odorless gas that makes up about 78 percent of the atmosphere. Some of it falls from the sky as a natural by-product of thunderstorms, some of it is converted by factories into fertilizer (the nitrates we mentioned that cause algae to bloom and choke waterways), and some of it wafts out of automobile tail pipes in the form of the greenhouse gas nitrous oxide. A gas with a sweet odor, nitrous oxide is sometimes called laughing gas. It may be used as an anesthetic by your dentist or as a propellant in aerosol cans. But in the water supply, nitrous oxide, like the other forms of nitrogen, is no laughing matter.

The U.S. government has set ten parts per million as the safe limit for nitrogen in drinking water. But over the years, drinking water supplies have been found to contain far more than that. In the Phoenix, Arizona, area, several water wells were shut down in recent years because they had levels of thirty to forty parts per million of nitrogen in them, much of it from automobile exhaust in the form of nitrous oxide.[12]

Pollutants also get into the water from melting snow. It may be difficult to accept, but snow, despite how lovely it looks on the ground, may hide chemical reactions that pour pollutants into rivers, lakes, and streams when the snow melts. Scientists call this process that accompanies thawing acid flush. In the winter, pollutants from the air become lodged in ice crystals and fall to the ground with the snow that has now formed; there the contaminated snow piles up in layers. These pollutants are kept from moving during the winter months because the snow acts like a freezer chest, keeping the pollutants in storage. But in the spring, the snow melts, and the meltwater starts to flow, carrying with it the contaminants that have been trapped in the soil and in the snow. As more and more pollutants are flung into the air, the acid flush is sure to become an increasingly serious problem. Scientists know that the meltwater is bad because of the masses of dead fish that often appear in many rivers right after the spring thaw. The polluted meltwater also affects the microbes that live in the underlying soil, reducing their numbers and thus upsetting the balance of the ecosystem.[13]

Pollution is not the only agent that is attacking our water and killing it. Dredging and draining are two other assailants. Dredging is the excavation of mud and rocks from the bottom of harbors and channels to clear them of debris and keep them open to shipping and boating. The muck is generally sucked out through huge pipes or hauled out on a long chain of heavy buckets. Draining is like draining water from your bathtub, only on a large scale it's done to reclaim land that's covered with water in order to build on it or use it for farmland. Boston's Back Bay section, with its many apartments and office buildings, is one example of reclaimed land, and on a much bigger, countrywide scale, the Netherlands, where several thousand square miles of land have been reclaimed from the sea, is another.

But while dredging has made shipping more efficient and drainage has given us more usable land, more shopping plazas, and more farmland, both practices are damaging to our water. Most often, the damage is noticeable in what we call wetlands. These are areas that include marshes, swamps, bogs, estuaries, and even prairie potholes. For many years, wetlands were regarded as Mother Nature's stepchildren, just worthless pieces of wasteland that could be made valuable only when they were dug out or dried out.

Now, however, scientists and environmentalists know that wetlands are valuable in their present state. For one thing, they are home for unique forms of plant and animal life. More than a third of the 600 species of endangered plants and animals need the wetlands to survive. Each marsh, for example, has its own special plants and grasses, such as the oyster grass that flourishes in salt marshes in Louisiana and the hairy marsh yellow cress, a plant now endangered in the state of Illinois. Other wetlands support beavers, ducks, and, as in Illinois, the endangered black-crowned night heron. The coastal wetlands of the United States are the spawning grounds — places where fish deposit their eggs — for up to 90 percent of the nation's catch. Even the prairie potholes that are found in the north central states are important, serving as nesting grounds for ducks and geese. Wetlands also help control floods and erosion of land by setting up natural barriers, provide timber from the trees that often grow in them, replenish underground water supplies, and even sop up pollutants from surface water.

As a result of drainage and dredging, the wetlands are shrinking fast. It is estimated that 300,000 to 500,000 acres of wetlands are disappearing every year in the U.S. Of the estimated 215 million acres that were here when the first Europeans landed, only 99 million acres remain.[14] The Mississippi Delta is a perfect example of wetlands dwindling away. Deltas are places at the mouth of a river where clay, sand, and gravel are deposited by the running water. The Mississippi Delta on Louisiana's Gulf Coast is one of the world's largest. It's called the Big Muddy because so much silt is piled up there. But dredging for canals, rerouting the running sediment to keep shipping lanes open, and building embankments, or levees, to control floods, have interfered with the natural buildup of the delta wetlands by preventing mud from settling there.

Along with the lack of new deposits of sediment, there is another threat to the Louisiana wetlands: the sea. As canals are built, salt water from the Gulf of Mexico pours easily and far into the delta's freshwater marshes. Grasses that thrive in the marshes cannot tolerate salt water and die.[15]

There is, of course, great concern over the wetlands crisis, and the protection of wetlands and the regulation of activities such as dredging are the responsibility of the EPA, the Army Corps of Engineers, and other agencies. Environmental groups have been calling for action to save the wetlands, and there have been many recommendations for tougher laws aimed at protecting these areas. But so far, there is no national wetlands management program, and the wetlands are still in danger because many businesses and politicians are reluctant to stop development in these areas. In the delta area we mentioned, the flood control and navigation projects are important to the area's economy. So, too, is drilling for oil in the delta, and the oil and gas industry provides much of Louisiana's income. Are the oil explorers, developers, dredgers, and drainers right? Or should we go all out to protect the environment, even though it means halting progress, putting companies out of business, and ruining the livelihood of workers and industries?

Water pollution, dredging, and draining are the main reasons our water is dying. And the more dead water we have, the less good water we'll have for our daily needs. Also, the more water we waste, the less water we'll have when we need it. Yes, we do have plenty of water, even with pollution as widespread as it is now. And although there are droughts and regional shortages from time to time — one drought in the 1930s lasted several years — as long as nature continues to function as it has always done, replacing what is sucked up from the oceans into the atmosphere as vapor with trillions of gallons of new water every day in the form of rain, we should always have plenty of water on earth.

But we do not always use it correctly. When we do not treat our water with respect and continue using it as a dump, when we squander it or draw more out of aquifers than is put in by nature, we could very well have a serious shortage someday. Even though water is not like oil, which will most certainly run out in the not too distant future, it is still vulnerable.

SOME SOLUTIONS

There are things that can and are being done to stop water pollution, protect precious natural resources such as the wetlands, and conserve water. Once again, the solutions require a commitment on the part of government and industry leaders, scientists, and ordinary citizens.

Laws, of course, can help, and it is essential that we strengthen our clean-water programs to make sure future generations have good water. Though there is still much work to be done, there has already been some improvement. According to the Association of State and Interstate Water Pollution Control Administrators, between 1972 and 1982, a period in which the U.S. population grew by 11 percent and the demand for water increased dramatically, the following heartening developments occurred:

> • 47,000 stream miles, a distance of about twice around the world, improved in quality.
>
> • 390,000 acres of lakes (about twice the size of New York City) improved.
>
> • 142 million people received better levels of sewage treatment, a 67-percent increase.
>
> • The total number of large municipal and industrial dischargers of water pollution who met their permit requirements almost doubled.[16]

Congress has revised and expanded the Clean Water Act several times, each time adding new requirements and strengthening its goals to include everything from pollution from pipes to pollution from agricultural runoff. On the other hand, laws don't always work, something we saw when we talked about lead pollution. In order for a law to stop water pollution, it has to be enforced as well as written and passed. According to one report in 1987, 36,763 public water systems committed more than 100,000 violations of the drinking water act, but state governments took only 2,500 formal enforcement actions and the federal government only fifty. Moreover, in 94 percent of the cases, customers were not informed of the violations.[17]

It is obvious that besides laws we need more aggressive approaches toward eliminating violations and a stronger emphasis on waste management and on eliminating pollutants at the source. Scientists must also develop better ways of recycling water, that is, treating wastewater to remove it of its toxic chemicals. When that is done, the water can be used again for irrigation. Israel, where few new freshwater sources are being found, now reuses 35 percent of its wastewater and hopes to be reusing 80 percent in a few years. New and less dangerous types of pesticides and fertilizers must be developed so that agricultural runoff will not be as serious a pollution problem.

We could also stop drilling for oil offshore or stop hauling it around on tankers. Unfortunately, these are more "Thou shalt not" kinds of solutions. Forbidding people to do things by law or from a pulpit does not always work. Indeed, prohibition is not always advisable, or realistic. Despite the arguments against offshore drilling, the fact remains that for better or worse, the U.S. still needs oil. So, how we drill, and where, are important questions to consider. We also must carry oil around in tankers. In 1990, President Bush announced a temporary halt, until after the year 2000, to several controversial drilling projects located off, among other places, the coastlines of Oregon, California, the state of Washington, and southwest Florida, and the rich Georges Bank fishing grounds off New England. Remember, though, that the halt is temporary, only a delay, and eventually, unless a permanent ban is ordered, some of those areas and others that have been called national sacrifice areas may be drilled for oil. Do you think some places should be given permanent protection from drilling? If national security becomes an issue — that is, if war or some other event disrupts our flow of oil — should we forget the ban and go ahead and drill?

There should be new limits on water use to prevent supplies from falling too quickly and improved irrigation systems that prevent a damaging accumulation of salts. According to the Worldwatch Institute, signs of what is called irrigation overstepping can be seen everywhere in the world. One of the most dramatic examples is the brackish Aral Sea, also known as Lake Aral, in the Soviet Union's central Asian republics; 95 percent of the Soviet cotton crop, a third of its fruits, a quarter of its vegetables, and 40 percent of its rice are grown in the region. Because of the dry climate in the region, 90 percent of the cropland is irrigated and, over the years, increasing amounts of water have had to be diverted from two major rivers that feed the sea in order to water the crops.

By 1980, the flow of water in the lower ends of the two rivers had been reduced to a trickle, and the sea had shrunk drastically. Not only that, but salt levels in the sea have tripled, winds pick up salt from dry areas and dump 43 million tons of it a year on the croplands, damaging them, and native fish species in the sea have disappeared. By the end of this decade, according to one expert on Soviet water issues, Philip Micklin of Western Michigan University, if nothing is done to correct the problem, the Aral Sea, once the world's fourth largest freshwater lake, "could consist of a main body in the south with a salinity well above the ocean and several small brine lakes in the north."[18]

Farmers sometimes overirrigate their crops because the price of water is either very low or free, or because they use cheap gravity systems — systems that rely on water flowing downstream from uplands or mountains. According to the World Health Organization, it is not uncommon for 70 to 80 percent of water drawn from a river to never reach the cropland. It runs off or evaporates before reaching the fields. Even in the Colorado River basin in the southwestern United States, the efficiency of water use is below 50 percent.[19]

Obviously, better management of water systems is needed. Unfortunately, this is not always easy to do, especially when it comes to groundwater and rivers. A number of questions arise. Who owns the water? Who should be given priority for its use in case of rationing — the farmers, or the people who live in the cities? Does a state have the right to tap into underground water or a stream that originates in another state? Can one person own a stream, or is it the property of everyone over whose land it flows? If a state government decides to build a dam across a river in their state, do the people downriver in another state have a say? The questions keep coming up in discussions of water rights, which are very complicated. In some states, people and communities own water, and they can trade it, sell it, or rent it. In others, it is not so easy to own water sources.

What do you think about the water supply situation? Should it be controlled, as, say, the use of the airwaves for broadcasting is controlled? Or should water be like the air, free for everyone to use? Would charging a lot for water make people use it more carefully? But what about poor people? Should they be charged for water, too?

Remember that most of us pay a bill every few months for water to be piped to our homes. We take that for granted, and for a great many of us it isn't generally all that expensive. And we waste water terribly. But in the developing countries of the world, many people — most of them women — have to walk for long distances in the drier regions to find water, then carry it back in jugs on their heads. When filled with water, those jugs can weigh as much as a suitcase you'd have to pay an excess baggage fee for at the airport. Sometimes, people in developing countries have to buy their water from vendors, who deliver it by bucket or donkey cart. In a typical shantytown, according to a recent report by the World Health Organization, the cost of this vendor service amounts to a fifth or more of the income of an average household. Thus, the poorest people, using the same amount of water as their better-off neighbors, spend more of their household budget on water.[20] If anyone knows the value of water, and how to use it best, it is the people who live in places such as India and Africa.

It is important that people have access to water, good water, because it improves health and hygiene. Providing a lot of water, though, is often costly. In many places there just isn't enough of it to run pipes into everyone's home. Where there is ample water, the terrain may be too difficult for water engineers to set up an efficient delivery system. Desalination, the process by which salt or brackish water is converted into fresh water, is one way water supplies may be increased. This can be done by distilling the water — vaporizing it in the sun or with fuel, then condensing it — or by removing the salt through other means. The problem is that the energy required to desalinate is expensive, and it is only in places where energy is cheap and water very scarce that desalting pays off.

We've talked about what scientists, politicians, industrialists, and farmers can do to protect and save water. What about us? As we will see next in our discussion of waste disposal, we can, for one thing, be careful about what we dump so as to prevent contaminants from getting into groundwater. Use nonhazardous alternatives at home as often as you can — baking soda for scouring powder and hot water instead of toxic drain cleaners if you're going to flush them down the drain.

To conserve, take some tips from America's Clean Water Foundation:

• Check for leaks. A dripping faucet with a one-sixteenth-inch hole allows 100 gallons a day to be wasted. Toilets are prime suspects. To check, simply drop some food coloring into the tank and wait fifteen minutes. If colored water shows up in the bowl, it's leaking.

• Use water-saving showerheads and faucets. Those high-flow showerheads that feel so great when you stand under them send water out six to ten gallons a minute. Flow-restriction devices cut the flow in half without reducing pressure.

• Water your lawn and plants early in the day to reduce evaporation and scalding of growing things by the sun. During the summer, water slowly and not as often. Avoid fine-mist sprinklers. You can also refrain from watering, and just wait for rain.

• When using a hose to water your yard or wash a car, put a pistol grip on it so you can shut the water off easily. Remember that a typical hose can deliver fifty gallons of water in just five minutes.

• Don't let water run continuously when brushing your teeth or drawing a glass to drink. An open faucet allows five gallons of water to escape in just two minutes.

• A full bathtub may be great to relax in, but it uses up a lot of water, so showers are preferable.

• Don't use the toilet as an ashtray, a wastebasket, or a food disposer. Flushing away six gallons of water to get rid of small amounts of solid waste is a very expensive form of waste disposal.

You also don't have to flush every time the toilet is used. "Save up" your flushes when you can.

Clean water, and enough water, should be everyone's goal. Like everything about environmental protection, we must all work together to achieve that goal.

5
THE PROBLEM:

TOO MUCH WASTE

If we could get cash for every bit of our trash, we would all be rich. The amount of trash that Americans, the most wasteful people on earth, throw away every single year is mind-boggling. The list includes: 16 billion disposable diapers, 2 billion razors and blades, 2 billion batteries, 1.6 billion pens, 220 million tires, 24 million tons of leaves and grass clippings, enough aluminum to rebuild the entire U.S. commercial airline fleet every three months, 12 million tons of glass, 3 million tons of steel, 50 million tons of paper, 10 million tons of plastic, and enough beverage cans to reach the moon 17 times if they were stacked on top of one another.

Altogether, every year Americans throw out 160 million tons of commercial and residential trash — that's 25 pounds per person per week — more than enough to bury 2,700 football fields in a layer ten stories high.[1] That's twice as much trash as Japan or Europe generates. Add in all the industrial nonhazardous waste and the oil, natural gas, and mining wastes, and it comes out to a total of 11 billion tons of nonhazardous solid waste a year — in the U.S. alone. Industry generates the greatest portion of what environmentalists call the waste stream, an estimated 7.6 billion tons.[2]

A lot of the waste that is dumped may, of course, be harmless, and indeed beneficial. For example, organic wastes — food and human waste — can be turned into fertilizer because bacteria in the soil and water cause it to decompose, to break down into a mixture called compost that adds nutrients to soil and improves its texture. But other kinds of common garbage can turn lethal. When any trash, household or industrial, is burned, it can send poisonous gases into the air for us to breathe. Buried in dumps, apparently safely tucked away, raw trash and the ash from rubbish that has been incinerated can turn into a soup of corrosive acids and other materials that seeps into groundwater supplies, contaminates drinking water, and pollutes farms. This soup, or garbage juice, is known scientifically as leachate. If the leachate is made up of very dangerous chemicals, all it takes is a single gallon of the stuff to make 100 million gallons of groundwater unsafe for drinking.

Industry is a large source of hazardous waste, just as it is a major polluter of the air. There are no reliable estimates of how much toxic waste the industrialized countries of the world produce. One estimate is around 375 million tons a year. Suffice it to say that the industrialized countries are the biggest producers of hazardous garbage. Billions of pounds of toxic chemicals are left over from manufacturing processes and must be gotten rid of, either by burying them somewhere (sometimes this is done illegally, in a site not approved for such dumping), incinerating them, or by pouring them directly into rivers, lakes, and streams through discharge pipes. For example, when paper manufacturers want to make their paper products snow white and remove impurities, they may bleach the raw pulp with chlorine. The process releases the chemicals we mentioned earlier, dioxins, and many other chlorinated compounds, which are often flushed into nearby rivers and streams. Companies that make petrochemicals — chemicals manufactured from petroleum and natural gas — also generate huge piles of dirty, smelly sludge in the process. Other culprits include metal smelters, where metals are melted down or extracted from ore; coal mines; cement plants; plastics factories; pesticide manufacturers; nuclear power plants; and factories that process fuel for nuclear weapons. There are laws that force industries to reduce the amount of waste they discharge, but many companies — among them those that drill for oil along the coasts and

discharge wastewater containing lead and other toxic materials —
still have permits allowing them to dump wastes into the lower end
of rivers, where they meet the sea.

The military, too, has dumped its share of hazardous waste, both
here and abroad. This recently became evident when the U.S.
removed some troops from Europe. Jet fuel, solvents used to clean
equipment, heating oil, ammunition, and chemicals used in training
soldiers how to fight fires — all of these have been turning up in
landfills and in the groundwater around the military bases.

Wastes are dangerous enough when they are released into the
water supply far from residential areas, but the situation worsens
when communities are constructed on top of heaps of waste, as often
occurs, or close to the dumps. The city of Woburn, Massachusetts, is
one such example. For more than a hundred years, tanneries, chemical companies, and a glue-making factory dumped their waste into
vacant lots, contaminating sixty acres with health-threatening lead, arsenic, and chromium. The companies had created a toxic time bomb.
Once branded as among the ten most hazardous sites in America,
Woburn had one of the highest cancer rates in Massachusetts: between 1969 and 1978, leukemia in children in the area was more than
double the national average.[3] Another disastrous result of waste disposal occurred in Elizabeth, New Jersey, in 1980. For years, residents
of the city had complained about the odors coming from a nearby
chemical plant. It turned out that thousands of barrels of explosive,
poisonous materials had been illegally hidden there. State environmental protection officials removed several thousands of the barrels,
but 24,000 remained. One night, the barrels exploded, sending a
gigantic fireball hundreds of feet skyward; fifty-five-gallon drums of
pesticides and acids were flung into the air, where they burst open
like bombs. Thirty people were injured, and the fire that roared
through the factory burned for ten hours before it was put out.[4]

The incidents at Woburn and Elizabeth were widely reported, but
it was New York's infamous Love Canal that became an international
symbol of the hazards posed by the dumping of toxic waste. Love
Canal was a Niagara Falls community that had been built up on land
once owned by the Hooker Chemical Company. There was a channel
there that the company had for many years used as a dump for chem-

ical waste. The channel was also used as a municipal waste dump. Thousands of tons of waste were deposited at the site until 1953, when the channel was filled in. Homes and schools were built on and around the channel, which came to be known as Love Canal. By 1955, hundreds of families were living in the area, and 400 children were enrolled in a new elementary school that had been built on top of the old dump. Sometime later, parents began complaining of sickening odors in the vicinity, of children being burned by chemicals, of explosions, and of black, greasy sludge oozing from the ground and seeping into basements.

Over the years, public health and environmental investigators, along with the residents themselves, turned up evidence of many different chemical compounds, some of them cancer causing, in the area. Heavy rains had also pushed leaking drums of deadly chemicals up out of the soil. But there was sharp disagreement over how serious a threat the chemical contamination actually was to the people of Love Canal. Some studies found higher than average incidences of miscarriages and of kidney, bladder, and central nervous system disorders. Others suggested that the people living in the area were at high risk of getting cancer or of bearing children with birth defects. But still others tried to play down the reports, suggesting that there were no serious health problems among the Love Canal residents. At one point, the situation turned ugly and some of the residents took two Environmental Protection Agency agents hostage for several hours. The hostages were released a few hours later, after the FBI ordered them freed, but the incident prompted President Jimmy Carter to declare a state of emergency at Love Canal. This allowed the government to evacuate the neighborhood and relocate 700 families living close to the canal. The federal government bought the homes, and eventually the company that had dumped the chemicals was held liable for cleanup costs estimated at around $250 million.

While this book was being written, the trial of the Hooker Chemical Company was underway in Buffalo, New York, and was expected to last six months. The company was being sued by the State of New York, which said that Hooker knew the risks when it dumped hazardous chemicals at Love Canal. The company's lawyers have argued, on the other hand, that the risks at the dump site had been exaggerated and that Hooker never intended to injure anyone. Moreover, Hooker's lawyers say, both the state and the federal government should share responsibility for the Love Canal incident. If the company is found guilty of knowingly ignoring the risks of dumping the chemicals, it could be assessed another $250 million as punishment.

The disagreement over whether the dumped chemicals had a significant effect on the health of the area continues still, a disagreement that surfaces almost every time some environmental disaster — from an oil spill to a railroad tank car explosion to a nuclear power plant accident — occurs.

There is another kind of industry, very unlike the Love Canal polluters, that also contributes to the frightening pileup of dangerous waste. Ironically, hospitals, doctors' and dentists' offices, laboratories, and nursing homes — places where the sick are treated and where the causes of disease are investigated — are at fault, too. According to the Environmental Protection Agency, thirteen pounds of waste a day are generated for every occupied hospital bed; other hospital studies say the rate is between eight and forty-five pounds per bed per day.[5] During the summer of 1988, medical debris — needles, syringes, vials, laboratory cultures, blood products, tissues, organs, and infectious bandages and sponges that had come in contact with patients with highly communicable diseases — reportedly began washing up on the shores of beaches all over the country.

On the other hand, a study by the Medical Waste Policy Committee, a national panel of industry and environmental experts, concluded that only 1 to 10 percent of the garbage that washed up on northeastern beaches in 1988 was medically related. Moreover, when the Center for Marine Conservation sponsored a cleanup program on New York and New Jersey shores during the fall of that year, the only medical waste items recorded were disposable syringes, and those accounted for less than one-half of one percent of all debris. In the Northeast, this waste and other debris came from sewer-system overflows and garbage that fell off barges on their way to New York's Fresh Kills landfill. Waste found on South Carolina and southern California shores was traced back to naval vessels. And in the summer of 1989 only a few incidents of medical waste on beaches were reported. It has also been argued that of the 3.2 million tons of solid waste that hospitals discard every year, only 10 to 15 percent is currently considered to be infectious.[6]

But whatever the amount, no matter where it came from or how much of it is infectious, the fact remains that medical waste is an environmental problem, and some of it is perfectly capable of transmitting disease. Even if medical garbage on the beach is just a horrible nuisance — as some people suggested that the odors and muck around Love Canal were — the fact remains that it doesn't belong there, no more than orange peels, empty beer cans, and broken bottles do.

We should emphasize that it is not just hospitals and industry that are to blame for the heaps of toxic waste. Every day, we contribute to the problem from our homes, and you'll probably be very surprised to know how much dangerous or potentially dangerous waste every one of us throws out. Most of the medical supplies that turned up on northeastern beaches in 1988 apparently came from households, something that many state and federal agencies neglected to address as they focused on hospitals as the culprits. People being treated at home for some ailment regularly dispose of bandages, unused medications, needles, and bodily wastes such as urine and feces, which can harbor viruses, including those that cause polio and hepatitis.

Then there are all those disposable batteries, the ones we pry out of our portable cassette players, hearing aids, watches, flashlights, and calculators when they run down. Household batteries, as small as they are, contain dangerous heavy metals such as mercury or cadmium. Deep inside landfills, they corrode, burst open, and discharge their toxic metals into the soil; when batteries are burned in incinerators with all the rest of the trash, the metals are released into the air to affect our lungs and our nervous systems. Automobiles also contribute to the pool of waste. Dead car batteries may not run an automobile anymore, but they're still a hazard when dumped because they are packed with lead and with corrosive sulfuric acid, which leaks out when the batteries themselves corrode. Used crankcase oil is also a common polluter. People drain it from their cars periodically and sometimes pour it into the ground or into the street, where it flows into sewers when it rains. Just one quart of it can ruin 250,000 gallons of drinking water.

We routinely toss out other seemingly harmless items. Here are just a few:

> • Mothballs. Most people dump these after clothes are taken out of storage. Mothballs are not as insignificant as they appear. They are made of a chemical with a jaw-breaking name, paradichlorobenzene, which can damage the liver and kidneys.

> • Paints and paint thinners. These items account for the majority of household hazardous waste, and a lot of cans containing substantial amounts of unused paint products go out with the rubbish. Lead and cadmium are among the dangerous ingredients put into paints.

> • Oven and drain cleaners, which contain lye, a very strong alkali.

> • Disposable pens and markers, which are full of hazardous solvents.

> • Baby powder, which often contains asbestos.

> • Detergents, many of which contain phosphates, chemicals that can soften water but can also kill lakes and streams.

If you start reading the labels on everything that you use around the house — from ant and roach sprays to cosmetics — you will become more aware of items that could be dangerous when they're thrown out as trash. For example, the label on a can of paint and varnish remover might read:

> CANNOT BE MADE NONPOISONOUS! Contains acetone, toluol, methanol, petroleum distillates, and methylene chloride, which have been shown to cause cancer in certain laboratory animals. Risk to your health depends on level and duration of exposure. Reports have associated repeated or prolonged occupational exposure to solvents with permanent brain and

nervous system damage. Intentional misuse by deliberately concentrating and inhaling contents may be harmful or fatal.

You may not know it, but two of the toxic ingredients in paint remover, toluol and acetone, are also found in something that many women use regularly: fingernail polish remover. And the next time you're planning to wash your hair, check out the label on that pretty little bottle of shampoo. Not all of the ingredients are toxic, but they certainly should make you realize that chemicals are filling your home. One bottle might contain — besides the more familiar water, sunflower oil, avocado pulp, cucumber juice, and peach extract — a variety of ingredients few of us can pronounce, let alone understand their purpose: sodium laureth sulfate, ammonium lauryl sulfate, dimethicone, tricetylmonium chloride, stearyl alcohol, cocamidopropyl betaine, divinylbenzene copolymer, methylparaben, methylchloroisothiazolinone, and ammonium xylenesulfonate. They might make your hair squeaky clean, but some of them don't do that to the soil and the water they probably end up in.

You certainly wouldn't drink paint thinner, nail polish remover, or shampoo, or rub them in your eyes. So why would you pour them carelessly into the ground or toss them out with your other trash to be buried in a waste dump where they can become part of toxic garbage juice? When possible, use them up, and when you dispose of them, do so according to the directions on the label; when in doubt, check with your local trash hauler. Fortunately, more and more manufacturers are substituting natural ingredients for some of the toxics they used to put into their household products, but a lot of dumps still contain materials from older products. For example, it wasn't until 1973 that manufacturers stopped putting mercury in cosmetics, hair tonics, and soaps, and the remains of many of those products may still be leaching out of the landfills where they were buried years ago.

What manufacturers have not stopped making, however, is plastics. Of all the countless things we toss out, none has created as much controversy as this familiar group of materials. Like pesticides and food additives and all the other chemicals that we must live with, plastics are both blessing and bane.

Plastic is a general term for substances that can be formed into a wide variety of shapes by applying heat or pressure. Plastic has an interesting history dating back centuries. Mixtures of glue and paper pulp that could be molded, called papier-mâché, were developed centuries ago in China, and while plastics are not made out of such materials today, one modern way of hardening plastic is derived from the method used to make papier-mâché. Another early form of plastic was the ceramic clay many primitive peoples used to make their cooking pots and dishes. But the history of modern plastics actually began in the late 1860s with the need to replace ivory, which was becoming scarcer and more expensive as herds of elephants were being destroyed for their tusks. A company that made pool and billiard balls out of ivory offered a $10,000 prize for a satisfactory ivory substitute. One of those who entered the contest was John Wesley Hyatt, an inventor from Newark, New Jersey. In 1870, Hyatt concocted a combination of nitrocellulose, a mixture made from wood or cotton pulp; camphor, an extract of the camphor tree; and alcohol. By heating the mixture under high pressure, at which point it could be molded, then letting it cool, Hyatt was able to make a very hard substance that came to be known as celluloid. Hyatt didn't win the prize, but his product became an enormous commercial success and was used to make dental plates, eyeglass frames, combs, and the men's collars that were in fashion at the time. Hyatt's celluloid was the first synthetic plastic made. Sometime later, cellophane — a transparent, thin film of cellulose — came along, followed by plastics made out of various combinations of shellac, soybean proteins, pitch, and coal tar.

Today, although a few natural plastics exist — rubber and resins among them — plastics are generally made in a laboratory out of various petrochemicals, along with pigments for color and other chemicals to make the plastic flexible, hard, or soft. Plastics may be molded into all kinds of tough material for use in everything from marblelike counter tops to automobiles, or they may be spun out into thin thread to make clothing, parachutes, and the material that surgeons use to stitch up a patient after an operation. You name it, and plastic plays a role: bathtubs and boat hulls and swimming pools; garbage bags, garden furniture, and golf clubs; drainpipes and drinking cups; milk bottles and toys, flowerpots and trash cans, refrigerators and skis and surfboards. Ninety-five percent of the large soft-drink bottles used in the United States are made of a light, shatterproof form of plastic. If ever a manufacturer needed an all-purpose material, it is plastic. Moreover, the wondrous qualities of plastic will probably be improved upon in the future. Already, Japanese researchers have developed a very tough superplastic, one that will stretch out for great lengths, like chewing gum, without breaking and which might one day be used to make long-lasting engine parts.

But plastics, for all their shining shapes and bright future, have a dark side. The more durable ones are made out of polyethylene, a petroleum-based product, and they are so durable that they may last for hundreds of years — a wonderful attribute if items made from them are used and reused by generations of families, but a nightmare as they pile up in waste dumps or wash up on shore after garbage is disposed of in the ocean. Sometimes the durability of, say, a plastic container becomes even more of a problem when the plastic is combined with other materials, as is often the case. Those compact and convenient square juice boxes that are so popular, for example, are made out of layers of cardboard, foil, and plastic, and as a result they are very difficult to recycle. In landfills, many of the plastics that do break down over time release pigments, fillers, and other materials used in their manufacture, and again, the leachate can contaminate the groundwater. Careless manufacture and incineration of plastics can send pollutants into the air. Workers who make plastics are at risk. In the 1970s, a number of factory workers involved in the manufacture of a vinyl plastic — a form used to make automobile seat covers, water pipes, rainwear, and credit cards — died of a rare cancer of the liver. The chemical in the plastic, vinyl chloride, or VC, had apparently been inhaled by the workers. Laboratory animals, too, have died of cancer after exposure to the chemical.

One familiar plastic that hangs around for a long time is Styrofoam, a material used to make beverage cups. Styrofoam, it seems, just will not disappear. Throw one of those foam cups into the ocean, and the polystyrene it is made out of — polystyrene is a material made of benzene, a toxic substance that also comes from petroleum — will fragment into many unsightly, tiny pieces that float. The foam is more than an ugly blight on the water. Many birds and ocean creatures mistake it for food, and when sea turtles, for example, eat it, the plastic's buoyancy prevents the turtles from diving, clogs their systems, and causes them to starve to death. The process by which Styrofoam is made also presents environmental problems. After the polystyrene has been formed, it is injected with gases — often the gas is the CFCs we mentioned earlier — to make it into foam.[7] And it is the CFCs, as we have seen, that play a huge role in tearing up the earth's ozone layer.

SOME SOLUTIONS

What can we do to keep the world from wallowing in waste, as seems sure to happen?

Well, we can bury it, burn it, or treat it in some way so that it shrinks and becomes harmless. We can dump it in the ocean, far from shore, or we can ship it out to some faraway country. We can blast it into outer space aboard a rocket and let it orbit some distant planet. We can reuse it. We can just stop producing so much of it.

Except for putting trash in orbit somewhere — which is not very practical because of the enormous cost of space shuttles, the awful thought of littering the cosmos, and the estimated 3.5 million pieces of space junk already left there by the space programs of the U.S. and the Soviet Union — each of these approaches is already underway. But each one, too, has its drawbacks and raises serious questions, as do the solutions that are offered for other forms of environmental pollution.

Before we discuss the options, let's consider a few questions you should be asking about waste disposal. For instance, should we force communities to accept a dump site even if means putting it close to people's homes? After all, the people of any town need a place to get rid of their garbage, and it has to go somewhere, right? It would seem, would it not, that we have to give something up if we want the benefit of waste-free homes. Is it not true that sometimes we have to do a little damage to gain something good? For example, burning trash might cause air pollution, but isn't that better than letting trash pile up all around us? Is it fair to send waste to other states? After all, some states accept garbage from elsewhere because they have more room and because they can use the extra money that they receive from dumpers. If they want to take somebody else's garbage, shouldn't that be their right?

And what about getting rid of waste in the ocean? If the ocean is so deep and so spacious, then is ocean dumping really all that bad? Doesn't the same hold true for shipping garbage out to areas of the world that are hardly inhabited, such as Antarctica? The space is there, so what's the problem? And since recycling is such a good idea, according to most environmentalists, why don't we just recycle everything? If science can put people on the moon and cameras into orbit, it certainly ought to be able to put every bit of waste to good use, right? Should we punish people who refuse to recycle garbage? And what about those tons of plastic that seem so hard to get rid of? Some of the things we make out of plastic may be safer than glass — plastic milk and shampoo bottles, for example, have prevented a lot of the serious cuts attributed to glass bottles — but is that enough reason to keep making so many items out of plastic? Why don't we just ban companies from making things out of plastic, or limit the kind of plastic that is used? Such a step may not be all that unusual. At this writing, the U.S. Senate was considering an amendment to the 1989 Solid Waste Disposal Act that would ban the use of cadmium as an artist's pigment. Besides its use in batteries, cadmium has long been a mainstay on the artist's palette, notably as the ingredient that produces vivid yellow and orange hues so essential to producing all those paintings of gorgeous sunsets and fall foliage. If enough cadmium gets into our systems, it can cause cancer and kidney poisoning.

Finally, why don't we crack down harder on companies that produce toxic waste? Some people say that factory owners and government health officials are more interested in playing down horror stories about toxic waste disposal than in alerting and safeguarding the public. Do you think the industries that generate hazardous waste and the companies that truck it off are only interested in making money and don't care about the consequences of all their dumping?

We'll address many of these questions in the pages ahead and, I hope, provide you with some information to help you answer them. But let's begin by saying that the situation is not as hopeless as it seems. Yes, there is a waste disposal problem, and yes, some of the rubbish is hazardous. But some things can be done, and are being done, to reduce the rate at which all that waste piles up. Let's look at the remedies and at the difficulties that sometimes arise when trying to implement them.

SOURCE REDUCTION. This is a fairly obvious way to prevent us from being choked by waste. It is also one of the most important. If we stop producing waste, or, as the environmentalists put it, practice source reduction, we can go a long way toward becoming a waste-free society. Many industries are already doing this, although we do not hear as much about it as we do about the discovery of an ancient waste site near a community. When a factory does not produce a lot of waste, it not only takes the pressure off waste dumps but it benefits itself because it avoids the risks and the high cost of treating or storing waste and of transporting it to a dump.

For a big company, reducing waste requires more than just doing something to trash — burning it, for example — as it's generated. Practicing source reduction means trying to find out just where in the manufacturing process waste is generated, then changing the process so that waste production is reduced. It means using different raw materials and maybe substituting safer materials for the more dangerous ones such as lead, cadmium, and chlorine. The Japanese, for example, have required battery manufacturers to sharply reduce the amount of mercury they put into the batteries. Companies could redesign their products, and, say, make plastics that are biodegradable, that is, are capable of breaking down in water and under the influence of various microorganisms in the soil. (Plastics are generally not biodegradable because they are made of molecules not found in nature, and few organisms are around that are able to feed on these non-natural molecules.) Or the companies that use plastic containers could eliminate them altogether. In 1990, the McDonald's Corporation announced that it would do away with its familiar plastic foam "clamshell" hamburger box and replace it with paper packaging. Companies might also make packaging, which accounts for a third of municipal waste by weight, more durable and thus able to be reused over and over. Some products could also be made more durable — rechargeable batteries, for instance, last far longer than ordinary batteries. Manufacturers could also sometimes use water instead of solvents to dissolve various substances. They could develop better equipment for rinsing out toxic chemicals after a product is manufactured or come up with new processes to recover and reuse waste material. (We'll discuss reusing waste later when we consider recycling.)

A number of companies have been successful in reducing waste at the source. One is the Minnesota Mining and Manufacturing Company (3M), which started a "Pollution Prevention Pays" program in 1975. By using fewer toxic chemicals, swapping safer materials for hazardous ones, and isolating wastes that can be reused, the company has cut waste generation in half. Every year, 3M eliminates 275,000 tons of solid waste, more than 100,000 tons of air pollutants, and 1.5 billion gallons of wastewater.[8] In 1989, 3M saved over $400 million because of its efforts. The company also explained the goals of its program to employees and gives awards to those who develop helpful projects. Another large firm, USS Chemicals, also rewards employees for coming up with waste-cutting ideas: at one point, the company had distributed $70,000 in rewards for projects saving a half-million dollars. Cleo Wrap of Tennessee, a manufacturer of gift-wrapping paper, virtually eliminated hazardous waste by substituting water-based for solvent-based ink, and in the Netherlands, the Duphar Company, which makes pesticides, decreased waste discharge by 95 percent by using a new manufacturing process.[9]

We mentioned that one way waste could be reduced is for companies to make plastics that are biodegradable. This is important because while plastic represents only around 7 percent of the trash dumped into landfills by weight, it takes up 30 percent of the space. One biodegradable plastic already in existence is the familiar cellophane. First marketed in 1924, cellophane is manufactured from wood and cotton pulp, which means that when it is dumped it decays just as leaves and grass clippings do. Because of this, a number of states have passed laws urging its use, and, thus, cellophane may become more widely used than it currently is.

Other biodegradable plastics are also being developed. Some contain starch, an important foodstuff that can be extracted from wheat, corn, rice, and potatoes. It degrades easily in soil to form water and carbon dioxide. The problem, however, is that many so-called biodegradable plastics made from starch only contain a small percentage of starch. The rest of the mixture is nondegradable polyethylene, which is made from petroleum. So when such a plastic is dumped, it does not decay completely. Thus, many of those garbage bags that are advertised as degradable in your local supermarket may not necessarily be doing much for the environment because when the starch decomposes the tougher pieces of the bag still lie around.

Researchers are trying hard to get around that problem. One U.S. company has been working on a plastic made entirely of starch and water, and another, in Italy, claims to have fabricated a plastic of starch and a substance, made from oil, that can dissolve in water. Still another company, in Britain, is developing a plastic made from a natural polymer that breaks down under the influence of bacteria and fungi in a few weeks.

One interesting research effort is going on at the Argonne National Laboratory in Illinois. The scientists there are trying to make biodegradable plastic from the billions of pounds of potato waste and cheese whey that are thrown away each year or used as cheap cattle feed. Half of all the potatoes that companies process to make French fries, hash browns, and instant mashed potatoes are never used. Whey, which is the watery part of milk that is separated out when cheese is made, is also discarded. The Argonne scientists convert the potato and whey waste into lactic acid with the help of bacteria and then change the lactic acid into a powder that is used to make plastic. The plastic is not only biodegradable, but photodegradable as well — that is, it can be broken down by exposure to sunlight. Besides being used to make drinking cups and yard waste bags, among other items, a degradable plastic like the one Argonne is working on could be used to make agricultural mulch films. These are plastic sheets that farmers use to cover their land to keep water in the soil and control weeds. Farmers today spend up to $100 an acre just to recover the nondegradable mulch film they now use. And if you think that we in the United States are the only ones who would benefit from a reliable, degradable plastic, consider how it could affect Hong Kong: the colony covers only 400 square miles but its residents and factories dump 1,000 tons of plastic a day, triple the amount thrown away in London.

Each of the research and source deduction efforts is commendable. But most of the biodegradable plastics won't be widely available for some time, and not every company is helping to reduce waste. In fact, only a few major industrial companies have taken steps to make any real difference; the rest either do nothing or make only a small dent in their waste piles. That is unfortunate because, as the EPA has noted, if more industries took the problem seriously, they could reduce the entire U.S. industrial waste stream by 15 to 30 percent.[10]

Can anything be done to make industry more responsible? Well, state and federal governments could impose heavy fines on manufacturers who do not make an effort to reduce waste at the source, or the manufacturers might have higher taxes levied against them. Or strict laws could be passed that would require companies to put reduction plans into effect. Certainly, the high cost of disposing of hazardous waste — from $20 a ton several years ago to $200 a ton today — has forced many manufacturers to come up with ways to cut down on the amount of waste they generate.

While such measures might make some manufacturers curb their waste output, sometimes strong prodding creates bad feelings. Some smaller companies might feel they are being unfairly singled out, or that they simply cannot afford the initial cost of revamping their way of doing business. Others might go along with the changes, but if they don't save money in doing so — or even perhaps spend more in the long run — they might be compelled to lay off workers or to cut back or eliminate some profitable product. Then, too, the United States already has a bewildering collection of state and federal rules and regulations in place. They apply to companies that produce toxic waste, the companies that treat, ship, store, and dispose of it, and the operators of dumpsites. With regard to medical waste alone, by 1989 twenty-two states had enacted new legislation or regulations addressing the problem.

Some people feel more rules and laws would only complicate matters and make doing business far more difficult. But without law we'd have chaos. Laws keep people honest. There is no question that the public's outrage over what happened at Love Canal compelled the U.S. Congress to pass a law in 1980 that created what is known as the Superfund program for cleaning up abandoned hazardous waste sites where toxic chemicals were disposed of improperly. Under the law, the EPA may clean them up itself if the responsible company refuses to pay for removing the hazardous materials and then bill the company for three times the cost. Thus far, of the thousands of contaminated sites nationwide, around 1,200 have been targeted for cleanup under the Superfund program.[11] The cleanup is expected to take decades, but without such a law it is likely that the hazardous waste problem would be even larger than it is.

Another way to get companies to eliminate waste before it gets out of the factory is to offer them something in return. For example, some states have established programs that provide technical assistance and equipment to help companies start up waste-reduction programs. It has also been suggested that the government should reward companies that reduce waste, either in dollars or by giving them tax breaks or low-interest loans for instituting programs that will reduce the flow of waste to dumps or incinerators.

But no matter which approach is chosen, each one recognizes that greater emphasis must be placed on lightening the enormous load of rubbish before it is produced. Indeed, environmentalists believe this must be the basis of any policy aimed at ridding the world of waste, hazardous or not.

Also, remember that it is not just industry that must stop creating waste. We all can do it. When shopping, for example, we can look for items that won't clutter the landscape. Accept paper bags if they are offered in your supermarket, or carry your own canvas bag, and avoid plastic ones. Choose eggs in cardboard packages over the ones in Styrofoam cartons. When you buy vegetables and fruit, put them loose in your shopping cart and not in plastic bags. If you use plastic bags, save them and use them again. Try carrying your own drinking cup to the fast-food counter so you won't have to use plastic. Buy things that you can reuse, and try to say no to disposables, as convenient as they are. If we all practice this kind of source reduction, we can lessen the load at the dump. As one environment-conscious organization, the Earth Works Group, has put it:

> If 10 percent of Americans purchased products with less plastic packaging just 10 percent of the time, we could eliminate some 144 million pounds of plastic from our landfills, reduce industrial pollution, and send a message to manufacturers that we're serious about alternatives.[12]

BURY IT. We've already mentioned the tradeoff of using dump sites. True, they're a place to dispose of our trash — but is it really disposed of when it's bulldozed under? Out of sight is not necessarily out of mind, or out of our lives. We've talked about the garbage juice that leaches out of dumps and gets into the water supplies. We've seen what happened at Love Canal and Woburn, Massachusetts, when toxic waste was discarded near communities. And even if the dumps were able to contain all our waste, what happens when the space fills up?

Already, landfills across the country are reaching capacity. In the U.S., 80 percent of solid waste is now dumped into only 6,000 landfills, and that number is shrinking fast. By 1995, according to the U.S. Environmental Protection Agency, half of our country's landfills will be shut down. Well, you might ask, why can't we just build new ones? We can, and we do. But ask yourself also, "Do I want one in my backyard?" (That question has inspired a movement known as NIMBY by its critics, for Not in My Backyard.) So many people are saying no to the question that the space available for new landfills is shrinking. Also, the landfills being constructed now will only be able to hold around four million tons of extra garbage a year, nowhere near the annual load that is trucked to the dump.[13] Unless far more dump sites are built, many cities and towns will be forced to ship their rubbish to distant places, a costly proposition that could turn out to be a waste of money if those sites are eventually exhausted. One state, New Jersey, is already sending 55 percent of its garbage to other states at tremendous cost, and other states are sure to be in the same situation. Worse, as landfills shut down, increasing amounts of rubbish will be dropped in illegal sites. This practice is going on even now. Recently, the owners of a private carting company were sentenced to twelve years in prison for dumping thousands of tons of medical waste and asbestos in an illegal landfill on Staten Island, New York. The landfill, it turned out, bordered housing and wetlands, including a breeding place for a family of wading birds known as white herons. The cost of cleaning up the area was estimated at $15 million.[14]

Whether we like them or not, landfills are necessary. Indeed, even if waste reduction practices became more widespread, we would still need new landfills because of the huge quantity of different products factories turn out and, unfortunately, because the public still seems to have an unquenchable hunger for more and more throwaway packaging. Many dumps bale and shred their rubbish, but these measures really only extend the life of a landfill. They do not make dumps unnecessary. Refuse, it seems, will always be with us, for it is the price we pay for living in the twentieth century and beyond. So, no matter how harmful, dumps are needed as part of well-managed waste-disposal systems.

Given that we must live with dumps, at least for the foreseeable future, there are things that can be done to improve them, making them more efficient, less of an eyesore, and, as we will see later, a source for something that we can actually use.

Years ago, dumps were often just huge, smelly holes in the ground, back lots, railroad embankments, or maybe swamps or secluded lakes. While town dumps existed, it seemed that you could dump your garbage anywhere you wanted to. All you have to do to see that is take a hike deep in the woods. Chances are pretty good that you'll uncover a trove of broken bottles, hunks of metal, old refrigerators, tires, car radiators, radio tubes, and the like. Some uncaring people still discard their rubbish wherever they can, but the laws that prohibit indiscriminate dumping are fairly strong. You can be fined for tossing garbage in a place where you should not — even for throwing a cigarette out the window of a car — because littering is just another, smaller version of illegal dumping.

Legal dump sites are, or should be, more than just holes in the ground. Plain old holes are often close to the groundwater level, and that, as we have seen, can be dangerous. To prevent contamination of the water supply by the leachate, dump designers now line landfills with clay or plastic sheeting that will contain the toxic juices. In Scotland, a gigantic, thick polyethylene bin liner is being installed to trap leachate. The liner will cover an area of sixty-six hectares (about 163 acres). Along with liners, engineers might install pumps that drain the leachate out to a treatment plant where contaminants could be removed. Sometimes, other chemicals are used to break the waste down to a harmless form. After treatment, what remains of the waste may be safely discharged into a nearby stream. The people who operate the modern landfills must also regularly drill holes right down to the below-groundwater level to sample the water and make sure that it is not contaminated — and they have to do this sort of checking even after the dump site has been closed for many years.

Such care is also being taken with stored gasoline, fuel oil, and solvents. Gas stations store gasoline in underground steel tanks, and chemical companies store their toxic substances, including pesticides, the same way. There are two million such tanks scattered around the United States, half of them at gas stations. According to the Environmental Protection Agency, several thousand of these tanks are corroded and leaking, and, therefore, are a threat to drinking water and public health. Just a single gallon of gasoline is capable of polluting a million gallons of water. In 1990, the EPA issued new regulations governing the underground tanks, requiring that the tanks be fitted with devices that detect leaks and that they be built to resist corrosion, and ordering immediate cleanup if there is a leak. The new rules should help protect the water supplies and, even if the equipment is so costly that it forces gasoline prices up, it would still seem to be worth the price.

But there should be another consideration when a modern dump site is constructed — its location. A dump site in anyone's backyard is not exactly a welcome gift. Aside from the health problems a dump can create, a waste site can reduce the value of all the homes near it. When you ask whether you'd like to be dumped on, ask whether someone else would like the same treatment.

All too often, as the NIMBYs — more often than not in affluent, white communities — argue against new dumps in their towns, waste sites, especially hazardous ones, are placed in communities with many poor, elderly, and minority residents. "The by-product of NIMBY is PIBBY (Place in Blacks' Backyard)," sociologist Robert Bullard of the University of California at Berkeley has said. Today, 60 percent of the U.S.'s hazardous waste sites are in the South, where a third of the nation's population lives. Moreover, three landfills near predominantly black communities in Emelle, Alabama, Alsen, Louisiana, and Pinewood, South Carolina, account for some 59 percent of the entire South's hazardous waste landfill capacity — although blacks make up just a fifth of the region's population. In Atlanta, 83 percent of the city's blacks live near uncontrolled hazardous waste sites, while only 60 percent of whites live in such areas. And blacks are not the only minorities who must suffer the sites. In Los Angeles, 65 percent of the Hispanic population lives near a toxic dump.[15]

BURN IT. This sounds like an easy solution to the waste pileup. After all, when you burn something, it pretty much disappears, leaving only thin, powdery ash behind. And ash is so fine that it'll just blow away, right?

Unfortunately, like many simple solutions, incinerating waste sounds better than it really is. First of all, every 1,000 tons of waste that is burned leaves as much as 300 tons of ash behind, certainly not a light package. So you'll still be left with a lot of waste that has to go to a dump, and although any reduction in waste is helpful, the dumps, as we have seen, are filling up fast, and it is difficult now to build new ones. Second, incinerator ash can be loaded with the dangerous chemicals and heavy metals we mentioned earlier, and when that ash is buried in unsafe dumps, the chemicals can leach out into the drinking water. Third, burning rubbish can spew some of those same toxic materials into the air, where they are spread over wide areas in all the smoke. And fourth, some materials, like the rubble from a demolished building, just can't be burned.

Despite those obstacles, since too much waste is generated for the amount of landfill space that is available, incineration is used to dispose of trash in many communities across the United States and elsewhere. And the number of trash incinerators is increasing. In 1970, only about 1 percent of all solid waste was burned; today, 10 to 15 percent is; by 1992, incinerators will eat up about 20 percent of the U.S.'s solid waste heap.

Unfortunately, some incinerator operators burn, or try to burn, everything that comes into the dump without sorting out items that could cause pollution problems or could be reused. For instance, when batteries are burned, they can shoot mercury-laden fumes into the air; the lead that flies out of incinerator stacks and into the atmosphere offsets the decrease in lead that deleading gasoline brought about; plastics that contain vinyl chloride produce dioxin and a poisonous, irritating acid gas called hydrogen chloride when they are burned; glass is not burnable, but when it ends up in an incinerator it fouls up the burning process and makes incineration less efficient. As one official of the Environmental Defense Fund in Washington has put it,

Incineration works, but on a smaller scale. If the philosophy is to burn everything, you only perpetuate the same problems we have now, by fouling the air with emissions and producing ash that contains toxic residues.[16]

A case in point is what happened in 1989 near Rotterdam, in the Netherlands. Scientists analyzing milk discovered dangerously high levels of toxic dioxins in the milk from 1,000 cows and laid the blame on an incinerator in the vicinity that burns 950,000 tons of domestic waste and 75,000 tons of toxic waste a year. The dioxins apparently came from the incinerator's smokestacks, were absorbed by the cows, and accumulated in their fat and then in their milk.

When trash is burned, two kinds of ash are produced. One is called fly ash, the fine ash carried out of the furnace by exhaust gases. Fly ash can contain heavy amounts of metals such as lead and cadmium. The other kind of ash is bottom ash. This is usually unburned, heavier stuff that collects on the grates at the bottom of incinerators, and while it is not generally as dangerous as fly ash, it often contains toxic junk. Both kinds of ash must be gotten rid of if an incinerator is to do its job properly.

To trap fly ash, incinerator designers install devices called scrubbers. These work by spraying a mixture of lime — the dry, white powder that goes into plaster — and water into the smokestack gases. This neutralizes, or weakens, the gases that would ordinarily produce acid rain and also cools them. In addition, the scrubbers help control the toxic metal particles that pour out of the stacks during the burning process by getting them to stick to the fly ash. Special filters capture the fly ash, which is then disposed of in a safe dump.

Unfortunately, many incinerators in the U.S. do not yet have adequate scrubbing equipment, nor do their operators properly sort out the materials that should be burned from those that should not. Among the countries that do a fine job of incinerating is Japan. For one thing, the Japanese carefully separate cans and bottles from trash that is to be burned. For another, Japanese incinerator employees are far better trained than those in the U.S., spending many months learning everything possible about how poisonous gases are formed. Even the way they dispose of their fly ash differs. In Japan, where 90 percent of the landfills refuse to accept household waste along with incinerator ash, fly ash is often mixed with cement, made into blocks or pellets, and placed in landfills fitted with liners and wastewater treatment equipment.[17] It is not uncommon for U.S. dumpers to mix fly ash, bottom ash, and ordinary garbage in a landfill.

There are a few alternatives to the usual kind of incineration, but many of these are in the experimental stage. One is to use sunlight to destroy toxic wastes. Scientists at one laboratory, the Solar Energy Research Institute in Colorado, have found that by multiplying the power of sunlight 1,000 times with a reflector they could create temperatures lower than those produced by conventional incineration but high enough to destroy dioxins. Moreover, the process leaves fewer toxic by-products behind.[18]

But while there are plenty of problems with incineration, it, like dumping, can be improved so that burning trash becomes less of a threat. Again, if waste is going to keep piling up, something has to be done with it, and incineration is, despite its drawbacks, essential if we are to deal with the trash crisis. Burning trash may not eliminate the need for dumps, but it would help to reduce the number needed.

RECYCLE IT. If you live in a community that is committed to

recycling, you are one of the lucky ones. If every community recycled — that is, reused its trash — we'd all be in good shape. The situation would be even better if recycling was employed along with
source reduction, well-managed landfills, and proper incineration.
That combination would remove an awful lot of trash from the waste
stream and would also reserve precious landfills only for junk that
could not be put to any good use.

Recycling does more than remove trash and improve the way a
neighborhood or a dump site looks. It reduces the enormous expense
of disposal and incineration, and it helps save natural resources —
our trees, fuel, and metals. Just consider how many trees are cut
down every week to produce Sunday newspapers: 500,000! By recycling aluminum, we save 95 percent of the energy required to turn
bauxite ore into aluminum from scratch. Saving all those natural
resources also makes us less dependent on imported raw materials.

Recycling also gives something back. It gives us a new resource,
something we can use to create a wide variety of valuable products.
Look at it this way: Recycled paper — and paper makes up about 36
percent of all solid waste — can give us newsprint, cereal boxes,
wallboard, cardboard, and toilet tissue. Just think of what we could
make out of the half a billion pieces of mail the U.S. Postal Service
moves every single day — most of which is eventually thrown away.
There is, in fact, enough wood pulp in 100,000 tons of typical rubbish
to make a gigantic roll of toilet paper, one that would wrap around
the earth ten times. Aluminum cans — a million tons will be disposed of in the U.S. by the year 2000 — can be recycled to make
more cans and lawn furniture. Steel cans can be used to make steel
for other products and to make tin. Discarded glass, which represents
eight percent of all our waste, can be remelted to make new bottles,
jars, and fiberglass. Plastic can be used to make toys and traffic cones,
flowerpots and drainage pipes, carpet backing, and fiberfill for pil-
lows, ski jackets, and sleeping bags. Your yard waste is good for topsoil, ground covering, and compost. Lead batteries can be made into
new batteries. Old tires can go into asphalt for road pavement and
roofing tiles, playground rubber mats, railroad crossings, and industrial fuel.

One of the more precious commodities that recycling can give us is energy. We waste a lot of energy in the U.S., just as we waste a lot of everything else. Every time we drive a car when we can walk, do not use storm windows when we heat our homes in the winter, or leave our lights or air conditioners on when we're not home, we are wasting energy. It just disappears, or flies out the windows, and once gone it cannot be recaptured — at least not in the way we might capture a fleeing butterfly with a net or water from an open spigot with a pail.

However, energy can be recaptured, in a sense, from garbage. Garbage is truly powerful — and not just in the strong odor that it gives off — and many communities here and abroad recycle it to generate steam and electricity. So powerful is trash, in fact, that our 160 million tons of annual municipal solid waste could yield 68 billion kilowatt hours of electricity when burned. Watts are units of power, and a kilowatt equals 1,000 watts. One kilowatt is the amount of electricity needed to light a 100-watt electric bulb for ten hours, while the average home uses between 600 and 750 kilowatts of electricity a month. Those 68 billion kilowatt hours lying there in all our garbage, then, would be able to light an awful lot of bulbs and run a lot of toasters, dryers, and television sets — considering that 68 billion kilowatt hours is the same amount generated by fifteen large nuclear power plants or thirty coal plants.

The process of transforming trash to kilowatts is called resource recovery, and it is accomplished at a waste-to-energy plant. There are more than a hundred such plants operating in the United States, and although we use only 6 percent of our rubbish to produce electricity — compared to West Germany, which ships more than 30 percent of its unrecycled trash to waste-to-energy plants — there is a growing awareness that converting trash to energy is better than just dumping it in a landfill or simply incinerating it, as long as the process is carefully controlled.

Using modern pollution control equipment (such as the incinerator scrubbers we mentioned) so that the environment will be protected, waste-to-energy plants burn waste in special furnaces. An attached boiler, something like that of an old-fashioned steam engine, produces steam from the hot gases and uses it to heat buildings or run a turbine generator, an apparatus that produces electricity.

Another way to turn refuse into fuel is to collect the gas that is generated naturally in the landfills. As bacteria digest the garbage, a rich gas called methane is produced. Also known as marsh gas, methane is the chief ingredient of natural gas, which is trapped in the earth's crust and is used as a fuel, and of coal gas. Methane is pumped from the rubbish heaps through pipes that are sunk into landfills and is used to fire boilers, run turbines, or serve as other forms of fuel. Tapping landfill gas not only gives us a product we can use, but it also prevents the gas from seeping out of the garbage to pollute the air.

Garbage decomposes slowly — lack of moisture often lets refuse lie around for twenty or thirty years without breaking down — and scientists are looking for ways to speed up the process and produce more landfill gas. Researchers at Argonne have found that by circulating water through landfills they can triple the speed at which rubbish degrades; this can boost the production of methane and make it possible to return the landfill to other uses in ten years or less.

Still another way to use garbage for fuel is to process it into pellets that can be burned to fire boilers and generate electricity. Mechanical sorters pick through a garbage heap and separate out the metals; the rest is pulverized, pressed into fuel pellets, then dried.

You would think that with all of recycling's potential for producing fuel and other useful products, it would be going on vigorously everywhere. Unfortunately, such is not the case. Only 11 percent of America's garbage is recycled, compared to 50 percent in Japan, where "waste not, want not" is a national obsession, and more than 30 percent in Western Europe. The Japanese are perhaps more conscious of recycling than we are because they live in such a crowded country and garbage is something they cannot afford to share their limited space with. (It should be pointed out, however, that even with Japan's admirable recycling record — along with nearly 2,000 waste-to-energy plants and 2,500 well-landscaped and efficient landfills — the Tokyo area alone will still have three million tons of garbage left over by the year 2005.)

Our poor record sounds even sadder when you realize that we are certainly capable of doing far better. Indeed, some studies suggest that up to 80 percent of our waste could be recycled, including by composting.

Granted, some U.S. communities do a better job of recycling than others. A few, in small cities, are up to 40 percent recycling, and many others have reached the 20-percent mark. Among the big cities, Seattle was, at this writing, the leader, with around 35 percent recycling and with 77 percent of the people in residential areas participating. Still others are trying hard — and the good news is that the number of states that require residents to separate recyclable items from trash, twenty-five at this writing, is growing. Maine hopes to recycle 50 percent of its solid waste by 1994, California by the year 2000; King County, in the Seattle area of Washington, wants to reach 65 percent recycling by 1994.[19] New York City, which generates 27,000 tons of municipal solid waste a day, started a program in 1989 with the goal of recycling 25 percent of all municipal waste by 1994. Even more ambitious, Connecticut plans to forbid the burning or dumping of any recyclable item after 1991 and will require that all newsprint be 90 percent recycled by 1998. California has a law requiring that all newsprint bought in the state have a minimum of 25 percent recycled fiber. Overseas, Italy expects to stop production of all nondegradable packaging material over the next ten years.

There are a number of reasons why recycling is not going on in every community. First of all, it requires the cooperation and enthusiasm of governmental leaders, manufacturers, various other businesses, and residents of a community — a mix that is not always easy to achieve. Recycling also involves several steps. Reusable items must first be collected, the most costly part of a recycling program, then separated. Many of the companies that supply newsprint have balked at recycling because of the expense of collecting old newspapers and shipping them to mills. In 1989, there were some forty newsprint mills in North America, but only eight or nine were using recycled paper to make new paper. (It's expected, however, that a couple of dozen or so will be able to recycle newsprint in the near future, and the industry is starting to spend large amounts of money on new recycling equipment.) After reusable items are collected, they have to be prepared for manufacturing, that is, they must be cleaned, shredded, baled, melted, powdered, pressed, or ground up. Then these intermediate products are used as raw materials to make new goods. Finally, the new products have to be sent back to the marketplace to be sold to consumers. Each of these steps needs many workers, and sometimes there is great disagreement over who should do what. Incinerator operators, for instance, do not often want the responsibility of separating out all the recyclable materials. Should it be their responsibility? The people who pick up the trash don't want to be the ones who must tell the homeowner what to recycle and how. Who should be doing that job? For recycling to be effective, it obviously needs someone to handle all that shredding, cleaning, and pulverizing of trash. But not many industries really want to get involved in this. And what if there aren't enough companies out there who will buy the processed trash and turn it into something useful? Wouldn't the processors be wasting their time? What about the consumers? Will they want recycled products? And though most people realize that landfill space is shrinking, is that enough of an incentive to go through all the bother of picking through our trash and separating each item? And what if a community has only so much money to spend in a time of economic distress, as is now the case? In New York City, for example, a huge budget deficit has forced the city to cut some services and lay off workers. The lack of money has delayed the expansion of the recycling program with its costly collection practices.

Concerns such as these have stood in the way of massive recycling programs in the U.S. It seems also that the states that have laws making recycling mandatory have the best participation; with a few notable exceptions, voluntary programs do not seem to do as well. Some communities give residents money if they recycle. For instance, in Rockford, Illinois, city officials pick out one household each week and check its garbage; if the trash doesn't have any newspapers or aluminum cans, the owner gets a cash prize of at least $1,000. Seattle gives free garbage pickup to residents who recycle and charges a fee for those who do not recycle.[20] In Japan, one community gives citizens weekly supplies of tissue paper, napkins, and toilet paper in return for their week's collection of newspapers.

In general, though, for a recycling program to be successful, it needs to offer more than cash or free goods. First of all, of course, communities have to have the money to start recycling. Recycling also needs to be convenient. That is, people are more apt to participate if they are given separate containers in which to deposit their cans, glass, newspapers, and plastic. Community residents are also more likely to go along if these containers can be picked up at curbside (as opposed to having to cart them to a central place) on the same day as the other garbage is collected.

Once you start recycling, if you haven't already, you'll find it very rewarding and very easy to do. Every one of us should not only recycle but should encourage others to learn more about the practice and do the same. You might want to conduct paper, plastic, or can drives of your own, or make it a class project. You'll make some money, help conserve our natural resources, and you'll probably feel good, too. No matter how small your recycling effort is, when it's added to what other people are doing, it will help protect your environment and make things cleaner for future generations.

DUMP IT IN THE OCEAN. Like burning and burying trash, ocean dumping seems to be a lot easier than recycling or stopping the production of waste before it gets started. After all, 71 percent of the earth's surface is covered by oceans, more than enough to handle our waste, right?

Well, maybe. Ocean dumping might be easier than recycling and source reduction, but it's certainly not better, nor smart. We've already seen what can happen when medical waste starts floating around on the water and then washes up on our beaches, when garbage juice leaks out into the groundwater, and when pesticides and other toxic chemicals flow out of factories and turn bays and rivers into a poisonous soup. And we know what happened in the Persian Gulf when millions of gallons of crude oil were deliberately pumped into the water.

Unfortunately, not everyone has heeded the warnings these disastrous events sent out. Waterways, as we have seen, are still convenient dump sites for polluters. To the dumpers, if they think about it at all, the ocean is a vast and bottomless well that will never ever fill up no matter what we do.

Ever since people have sailed the seas or lived near them, they have deposited their waste in the deep, and not so deep, waters. Ocean dumping, which includes depositing trash in rivers, since they carry waste to the sea, has long been viewed as an easy, inexpensive way to get rid of trash. Many cities still legally send sewage sludge out into harbors through pipes or haul it out in barges and drop it off the coast. In the New York–New Jersey area, dumping of sludge increased from five million tons in 1973 to nearly eight million tons in 1986.[21] (New York City and a few other sewage authorities in New York and New Jersey are the only ocean sludge dumpers in the nation. Such dumping is supposed to stop under Congressional order by 1992.) Britain drops nine million tons of sewage around its coasts every year, most of it in the North Sea. Worse even than all that, huge, trash-carrying ships that cannot find an appropriate legal land-fill for their noxious cargoes or do not have permission to dump gar-bage in the ocean still jettison tons of hazardous waste far out at sea, the captains hoping they won't be caught and fined.

Much of what goes into the ocean is, of course, the waste that the crews and passengers generate and that ships must get rid of. Other times, the discharge is accidental, or just careless. Ships sink, carrying everything and everyone aboard down with them. People die aboard ship and are buried at sea, or they fall overboard and drown. Organic material — including people — is, of course, absorbed by the ocean. But passengers and crews toss their beverage cans and cigarettes and food scraps overboard; oil tankers flush the residue of their grimy, greasy holds into the water; warships send rockets and bombs into the ocean during gunnery exercises; planes crash into the sea from the decks of aircraft carriers; fishermen throw away or lose millions of pounds of fishing gear. It is this sort of debris that piles up in the ocean.

Whatever the source, flotsam and jetsam, it seems, are every-where, fouling once-unpolluted expanses of water from the Antarctic Ocean to the South Pacific and killing marine life. Looking at the messes that increasingly appear off our own shores, in the Atlantic and the Pacific, one cannot help but feel that the lovely words of "America the Beautiful," "from sea to shining sea," are but the figment of a songwriter's imagination.

Whether ocean dumping is legal, illegal, or accidental, the fact remains that the world's water cover is a common resource that must be protected. Although your geography teacher will tell you that there are many oceans, the fact is that all of these oceans, nicely divided up into Atlantic, Pacific, Indian, and so on, are really one large body of water, a single ocean. Thus, what we dump into one ocean is an assault on another, no matter how far away. There are no concrete walls separating the Atlantic Ocean from the Mediterranean Sea or the Pacific Ocean from the Indian Ocean, and trash that is floating or sunk in one may eventually wash up on the shores of the other. Wind and waves, currents and tides, will see to that.

Some waste — foodstuff that is eaten by fish or degrades easily, or most spilled oil that evaporates over time — can be handled easily by the oceans. Water has the natural ability to wash itself clean. The oceans, in fact, can take a lot of punishment by absorbing pollutants, and they can even make a comeback when they are hit hard. But, as was said in the chapter on dying water, there is only so much a body of water can take and only so much it can do to regenerate itself, especially if dumping continues without any letup.

Sterner laws and treaties are one way nations try to stop ocean dumping of materials that the ocean has trouble with, things like plastics, toxic chemicals, and various other forms of industrial waste. In 1987, the U.S. joined twenty-eight other nations in approving an amendment to a treaty known as Marpol (for marine pollution) that bars vessels from throwing plastic of any kind into the ocean. Given all the merchant and naval ships out on the high seas — they have dumped tons of plastic over the side every day of the year — one has to wonder whether the treaty will make a difference. Laws and treaties might stop massive dumping, but they'll probably do little to prevent individual sailors either on large ships or small fishing boats from tossing bags of trash overboard whenever they feel they can get away with it. And, like individual votes that can decide an election, every bag counts — every one adds to the waste pool.

So, while some laws are in place or about to take effect, and despite the promises by national leaders and various international agencies to ban all ocean dumping, the practice goes on still, and so does the debate over whether the oceans are a good place to dispose of our waste.

Today, the carrying of waste by ships or barges to designated marine disposal sites in deep water far out at sea is regulated by the Marine Protection, Research, and Sanctuaries Act, usually referred to as the Ocean Dumping Act. The waste that is dumped into the oceans includes sediments dug out of rivers and harbors during dredging operations, industrial waste (including alkaline, acid, and pharmaceutical waste), and municipal sewage sludge, which is generally 95 percent water. Fines may be imposed if barges dump in shallow water closer to shore than the designated sites or if floatable materials are thrown out with the acceptable rubbish.[22]

Why is ocean dumping allowed? Besides the long history of ocean dumping and the convenience of the practice, the fact that ocean dumping is inexpensive compared to other options is an important part of the debate. As marine scientist Kenneth Hinga and oceanographer John Knauss of the University of Rhode Island's Graduate School of Oceanography explain it:

> If the ocean option is removed, governments will either need to increase taxes or forego spending on other deserving needs if they are to support more expensive options. Arguments about how to distribute these costs should not be minimized. Our society has limited resources. How much are we willing to pay to have a cleaner and less risk-prone environment? What other needs will we neglect?[23]

Ocean dumping also continues because no one can really predict what happens to the water and the creatures that live in it when trash is tossed overboard. We've already seen, in our discussion of water pollution, what can happen sometimes with some forms of waste. But, as the Rhode Island scientists see the difficulty of predicting the precise effects of waste disposal:

It is a question that must be asked separately for each type of waste. Each has its own characteristics. To further complicate matters, the answer may be different for different bodies of water. In some cases, we are currently able to predict the fate and effects of different chemicals with a high degree of confidence. Through the last few decades we have learned a great deal about marine pollutants. We have learned from experiences with pollutants in the environment and have greatly increased our understanding of the individual processes which ultimately control the behavior and effects of pollutants. In other cases we do not understand the characteristics of marine organisms, the properties of the potential pollutant, or interactions in the ecosystem well enough to make reliable predictions. It is not always easy to know when scientific evaluations are on firm ground or quicksand.[24]

We really can't prevent ships carrying toxic materials from sinking in a storm and littering the ocean bottom or, in the case of war, from going down in a battle. But we can stop the overuse of the seas for trash bins. If we cannot stop the practice entirely, perhaps we can at least be more careful about what kind of waste is dumped at sea, and where. After all, if the ocean is going to be used as a dump, it should be given the same attention we give the landfills when we try to make them safer.

SHIP IT OUT. That has been done, and it is still being done. In 1987 and 1988, three million tons of hazardous waste were transported from the U.S. and Western Europe to countries in Africa and Eastern Europe. Some of the ships carrying waste cargoes were like the infamous *Pelicano,* a ship that for more than two years in the late 1980s sailed around the world seeking a port that would accept the 14,000 tons of incinerator ash that had been loaded on in Philadelphia. Like the journey of the spectral *Flying Dutchman,* the legendary ship condemned to ply the seas forever, the *Pelicano* sailed on and on, denied permission to empty its holds by every country it approached. Finally, the ship dumped 4,000 tons of its waste cargo off a beach in Haiti, then slipped back out to sea amid reports that it was illegally dumping the rest of the waste in the ocean somewhere. Sometime later, off Singapore, the *Pelicano*'s skipper announced he had unloaded the ash in a country he refused to name.[25]

Waste is shipped from industrialized countries to the Third World because so much trash is piling up with no place for it to go and because of the high disposal costs at home. In the U.S., it costs from $250 to $350 a ton to get rid of hazardous municipal and industrial waste, but some developing countries will accept it for as little as $40 a ton.[26] Many of these countries take the waste because they are strapped for cash and are willing to take their chances with poisonous garbage. Other times, hazardous waste is just dumped without permission or through illegal deals between waste contractors in countries that want to dispose of the garbage and corrupt officials in the countries that will receive it. Just such an arrangement occurred between 1987 and 1988 when 3,800 tons of toxic waste were shipped from Italy to a small port in Nigeria and dumped illegally. The waste contained at least 150 tons of the notorious PCBs.

No matter how and why waste gets to Third World countries, it is a bad trade. For one thing, many of the countries that accept hazardous waste are not equipped to handle it. Few of the countries have regulations to control how they handle their own output of hazardous waste, let alone that of others. These countries also lack the technology to dispose of waste. Even when foreign contractors build plants in Africa or Asia, they fail to include the costly waste-disposal systems. And where new technology is available, it is often not up to the job. In Lagos, Nigeria, for example, five new incinerator plants were standing idle for some time because they could treat only garbage containing less than 20 percent water; most of the city's garbage is 30 to 40 percent liquid.[27]

Another problem with sending hazardous waste to developing countries is that the environment cannot handle it. Many Third World countries are in tropical areas, and the frequent rains and poor soil there allow chemicals to flow out easily into the groundwater. As Saad M. Baba, third secretary in the Nigerian mission to the United Nations, has observed, "International dumping is the equivalent of declaring war on the people of a country."[28]

In 1989, representatives of 105 nations agreed to tighten restrictions on international shipments of waste. While the agreement will not ban waste exports altogether, it declares that no waste can cross national lines unless environmental precautions are taken and the government of the importing nation gives its approval.[29]

All of the solutions to the waste disposal problem that we have offered have, as you can see, some flaw. We must understand two things, however. One is that we will never be without waste and, two, there is no single effective way to dispose of it. Acceptance of those two facts leaves us but one approach, and that is that we must employ many approaches — even the ones that we do not like at all because they may be offensive, may create other problems, or are too expensive. There is no such thing as a free lunch. If we want to live on this earth, we have to be willing to make trade-offs, to compromise on occasion. This does not mean that any trade-off will do. When you consider all the options for disposing of our waste, think about which ones would work best combined and which combination requires the least compromise. Perhaps you'll come up with something the experts have not considered.

6
THE PROBLEM:

RADIATION POLLUTION

On April 26, 1986, a huge explosion and fire at a nuclear power plant at Chernobyl, near Kiev, in the Soviet Union blew massive amounts of radioactive materials high into the air. The accident, the worst disaster in the history of nuclear energy, had a horrendous effect on the health of people living in the area and on the environment. At least thirty-one people were killed — some officials believe the number was actually in the hundreds — and countless thousands were seriously exposed to the radiation.

While we may never know just how much radiation the population received from the blast, there have been estimates — and they are not encouraging. A few years after the accident, the Soviets revealed that radiation exposure was far worse than had been originally believed. For one thing, heavy amounts of radiation were found more than 200 miles from the explosion site and in places originally thought to be safe. Moreover, some four million people were found to be living on contaminated land, and the thyroid glands of more than 150,000 people were "seriously affected" by doses of radioactive iodine, an element that is a component of fallout. (The thyroid, in the base of the neck, controls how we convert food to energy and also traps iodine in the bloodstream.) The Soviet authorities also said that the projected rates of thyroid cancer were far higher than normal for the population and that the death rate for people who had been working at the nuclear plant since the accident was ten times what it had been before the accident.[1]

The tragedy at Chernobyl fulfilled the worst fears of those who are opposed to the use of nuclear power as a source of energy. After the accident, thousands of Soviet citizens marched in the streets demanding that the government leaders be arrested and tried for not having told people about the dangers of the accident. More protests followed, these against the building of any new nuclear power plants.

Such protests, as you know, are common occurrences any time a new plant is to be opened or planned in the United States and in other countries that rely on nuclear power to provide electricity. Many people are worried about, and intensely afraid of, nuclear power and of the special kind of waste is produces. In this country, the antinuclear forces had much to demonstrate about in 1979 when a scary accident occurred at the Three Mile Island power plant in Pennsylvania. The incident involved what nuclear engineers call a near meltdown, a partial collapse of the inner workings of a nuclear plant. A full meltdown occurs when the nuclear fuel in the plant's reactor — the device that produces the nuclear energy — overheats and melts. So intense is the temperature that the reactor collapses and burns down right through the plant's foundations, an event that has been called the China Syndrome, so named after the familiar joke about digging a hole so deep that it will come out in China. A full meltdown did not occur at Three Mile Island, but the accident released radiation into the air, enough to warrant studies about health risks to people living in the area. Moreover, ten years after the accident, there was still evidence of radioactivity in the lower portions of the reactor.

Nuclear energy, like chemicals and coal, can be both good and bad. Nuclear plants can supply us with plenty of electricity without our having to rely on dwindling supplies of fossil fuel, and they have the potential of doing so without throwing pollutants into the air as coal and oil do. Nuclear medicine, the use of various forms of radiation to cure and diagnose disease, is an important branch of the healing arts. And no matter what you may think about nuclear weapons, they are a fact of life in modern warfare and, indeed, may well be an important deterrent to another world war.

But nuclear power has its down side, too. Accidents can happen, and as we have seen at Chernobyl and Three Mile Island, they do on occasion. Moreover, when a nuclear accident occurs, it has the potential for creating an enormous amount of damage to life and the environment. The fallout from the Chernobyl blast even turned up in the once-pure snow of the Antarctic almost two years after the accident, apparently having crossed the equator to get there. Military veterans who were observers of the many U.S. nuclear weapons tests in Nevada regularly seek compensation from the government for cancers they believe were caused by the blasts. Atomic bombs, for all they do to help keep the peace, are terrible weapons of mass destruction with explosive power equal to many thousands of tons of TNT. The two bombs the United States dropped on the Japanese cities of Hiroshima and Nagasaki at the end of World War II killed more than 100,000 people and left hundreds of thousands of survivors radiation-poisoned and doomed to slow deaths from all sorts of cancers. Even today, more than forty years after the bombs were used, many of the survivors remain in hospitals suffering from far more physical ills than the rest of the population.

There is no doubt that radiation is a polluter of monumental proportions. From the fallout from bomb blasts and weapons tests to power plant accidents to the radiation that seeps from the earth's crust during oil drilling operations, radioactivity is a destroyer of the environment. And these are not the only sources of radiation with a fearsome side. We are exposed to other potentially dangerous kinds of radiation almost every day — electromagnetic fields from overhead power lines; rays from microwave ovens, television sets, and computer screens; radon gas that rises naturally out of the ground and gets into our homes through cracks in our basement floors; radiation from electric blankets and sunlamps, from beepers and pagers that we wear on our belts, from dental and medical X rays, even from food that has been irradiated to make it last longer on the shelves.

And along with all this radiation comes another problem: what to do with the waste products left over when radiation is harnessed to do some job for us. Everything we do, as we saw in the last chapter, leads to the generation of some kind of waste, from the smoke that pours out of an incinerator to the hair that ends up on your barber's floor to the remains of a fast-food meal. The nuclear industry is no exception. Waste from weapons tests, from power plants, from hospitals, even from our homes, must be disposed of, and disposed of safely and efficiently. But it is not something we can do easily, as we shall see, just as it is not always easy to dispose of our ordinary household and industrial waste. Before we look at the disposal problem, let's turn for a moment to the nature of radiation and to some of its many troublesome sources.

There are many types of radiation, each one occupying a place on the range-of-energy ladder, the electromagnetic spectrum. Radiation includes the immense energy that we associate with nuclear power and the atomic bomb, the kind that occupies the high end of the electromagnetic spectrum. In the middle and lower frequency end of the spectrum are the other, weaker forms of radiation — ultraviolet radiation, light, infrared radiation, microwaves, and radio waves.

One way that radiation is produced is when the nucleus, the core of an atom, of certain elements disintegrates. Elements that can lose weight and give off invisible rays this way are the heavy, unstable elements; they are the ones we call radioactive. The rays that they emit are on the high end of the electromagnetic spectrum and are named alpha, beta, and gamma. Alpha rays are the weakest, and the least penetrating, of the three forms of radiation produced by radioactive elements; they can be stopped by a sheet of thin paper or tinfoil. Alpha articles are dangerous only when they are inhaled. Beta rays are the most common of the rays and are more penetrating than alpha rays. Gamma rays are small but very intense and are the most penetrating of the radioactive emissions. Another thing to know about radioactive elements is that each one decays at a certain rate. The time it takes for a radioactive element to decay to one-half of its original strength is called the element's half-life. Put another way, we can say that radioactive elements have a built-in clock that determines how long they'll live. Some elements have a half-life that is measured in seconds; others, like beryllium, a half-life of millions of years. Uranium, a very long-lived element, has most of its atoms flying about for billions of years!

Not all elements give off all of the rays we mentioned. Uranium, for example, gives off alpha rays, while radium gives off alpha and gamma rays. Some forty of these radioactive elements are found in nature — uranium, radium, and thorium among them. Others may be made in nuclear reactors or in huge pieces of laboratory equipment called accelerators. Among these are plutonium, which is produced from uranium and is used as fuel for nuclear reactors and the atomic bomb.

Every day, each one of us — humans, other animals, and plants — are routinely exposed to a kind of radiation called background radiation. This is a part of our environment, and it comes not from nuclear reactors or weapons tests but from two other sources. One source is outer space, in the form of cosmic rays. These are believed to have been produced by supernovas, or exploding stars, and by the time they reach us from so far off they have lost so much strength that they pass harmlessly through our bodies. The other sources of natural radiation are some very common materials — gamma rays and X rays are created by the decay of potassium and carbon in our bodies and of uranium, thorium, and other radioactive elements in the soil. (X rays are also generated by the familiar machines in hospitals and dentists' offices.)

Some places such as Brazil and India have very high levels of natural gamma ray activity in the soil. Plants, fruits, and vegetables that grow in those countries are often radioactive as well, and when people eat what is grown in regions with high levels of background radiation, they are at some risk. The Brazil nut is one extreme example. This tasty snack food has a very high radioactivity — about 14,000 times that of ordinary fruits! Cereals, too, are fairly high in radiation, with 500 to 600 times more natural radiation than fruits. Cattle and cows that eat plants in highly radioactive areas can also pass on the high levels to people in meat and milk. Some parts of the world also have more radiation in their drinking water than others because of radium and other radioactive elements in the soil.

One natural source of radiation that has caused a good deal of concern lately is radon. It may account for half the radiation we in the United States are exposed to. Radon is a colorless, odorless gas that is formed from uranium in rocks and soil. As uranium decays, it changes into radium, which gives off radon gas. When this gas comes out of the ground through cracks and remains outdoors, it usually disperses in the air and doesn't cause any problems. But quite often, radon gas stays underground; it flows along there for miles until it finds its way into people's homes through cracks in the floors and foundations, even coming in through walls and sewer pipes. (Radium also seeps into the groundwater and may come up in wells. Also, when workers drill for oil, radium-tainted water may be pumped up with the oil. Years of drilling have caused widespread radioactive contamination of oil fields everywhere in the United States.)

Some areas of the country have more radon gas than others, and millions of U.S. homes have levels above that considered safe by the EPA. A few years ago, technicians found the highest concentration of radon gas in the United States in a Pennsylvania town. When they took air samples at one home, they calculated that by living in the home for one year the owners had been exposed to the equivalent of 455,000 chest X rays![2] Because radon has long been known to contribute to lung cancer, especially among uranium miners, the owners of the home were probably at increased risk of developing lung cancer.

Other than natural sources of radiation, there are the forms of radiation that we are exposed to when we go to a hospital or a dentist. One way we are bombarded with radiation is with X rays. These rays are on the upper end of the electromagnetic spectrum. They can penetrate tissues and enable us to see a picture of the bones and organs inside our bodies. Some 300 million Americans have X rays every year, and many others have more elaborate forms of diagnostic radiation. One of these more sophisticated tools is called a CAT scan. This stands for computerized axial tomography; it involves a combination X-ray machine and computer that revolves an X-ray tube around, say, a person's head. The result is a three-dimensional video image that shows details that an ordinary X ray cannot. Other forms of diagnostic radiation include MRI, magnetic resonance imaging, which uses magnetic fields and radio waves to scan our insides with even more clarity than CAT scans, and PET, for positron emission tomography, which uses small amounts of radioisotopes (radioactive variations of different elements) to measure blood flow through a patient's tissues and to determine if his or her biochemical processes are working correctly.

Radioactive iodine is another diagnostic tool. When a doctor suspects a person has a thyroid problem, the patient is given a drink containing a tiny amount of the iodine isotope. A healthy thyroid gland is able to prevent the iodine from entering the bloodstream; doctors can tell that the thyroid is not functioning properly if it fails to retain the iodine. Various forms of radiation are also used to treat a number of diseases, among them cancer; lasers, which are concentrated light rays, are routinely used to perform surgery and remove blemishes from the skin.

Another way we take in radiation is through food. Irradiation is a method of preserving the freshness of food. Food is exposed to carefully controlled doses of X rays, just as the human body is examined with X rays. Opponents of this process argue that it is not safe, and they cite studies that irradiated food causes cancer and various genetic defects in laboratory rats. Moreover, they complain that the process destroys vitamins and other nutrients. Maine has banned the practice of food irradiation, and other states are considering doing the same, at least until further studies can be done. However, an international committee of experts of the World Health Organization is satisfied that irradiated foods are as safe as foods processed by other methods, such as heat treatment and chemical additives.

Food irradiation and nuclear medicine set up more of the same conflicts that have arisen throughout this book. X rays and the other forms of radiation used in medicine are essential diagnostic tools. On the other hand, they can be hazardous to one's health. Do we stop using X rays, CAT scans, and radiation therapy altogether because they are potentially dangerous? Or do we continue to use radiation as carefully as possible? Without X rays and the other forms of medical radiation, what would we do?

Insofar as food irradiation is concerned, there are other alternatives. But is that enough reason to ban the process, particularly if many scientists believe that it is not dangerous? Do not the benefits to public health — irradiation kills microorganisms and insects that could be very harmful to us — far outweigh the risks?

What about the other forms of radiation we mentioned, the ones in the middle and low end of the spectrum? Are they dangerous, too? Possibly. Take electric power lines, those familiar wires that run over our streets and along our highways. Both they and household appliances — toasters, electric blankets, and so on — generate low-level electromagnetic fields that have long been suspected of causing cancer, including the blood cancer leukemia. While a direct link has not yet been proven, a preliminary report by the EPA in 1990 concluded that there was enough evidence of a possible connection to justify more research into the matter.

It would be irresponsible at this stage to say we're all in danger every time we pop bread in the toaster or walk under power lines. Scientists still don't know how radiation of this sort might cause cancer; the low-frequency electromagnetic waves do not appear to work on the body's cells in the same way as radiation from X rays and the other heavy rays. Moreover, the fact that most of us are exposed to toasters and the like for only very short periods of time is a hopeful note. But still, given the link between other forms of radiation and sickness, the possibility that low-frequency radiation might present problems has to be taken seriously.

The same holds true for the use of VDTs (the video display terminals our computers require), television sets, microwave ovens, and even the beepers and pagers we use to receive messages. Each emits various kinds of radiation which, in excess, could pose problems for the user. The radiation levels, however, are very low, and with the proper precautions — in the case of VDTs, for example, limiting the number of hours and using a shield to filter out harmful rays — it is doubtful that an individual would be subjected to a significant health hazard. Again, be aware that while these forms of radiation are not powerful enough to do what their cousins higher up the energy ladder can do, they are still able to damage our eyes and skin and cause headaches, among other problems, and might well have some connection to reproductive disorders, even cancer.

All of this of course raises the question of how much radiation is too much. A hard answer is that almost all radiation is capable of causing damage or making us sick. From the blinding light of a welding torch to the skin-blistering heat of a sunlamp to the cellular damage created by radiation fallout, radiation is not something to take lightly. Even background radiation and the radiation we absorb from food and water, which may not be dangerous by themselves, can increase the risk of illness when they are combined with other sources — perhaps a nuclear reactor or a weapons plant in the neighborhood, or too many medical X rays over a short space of time.

Scientists have been feuding for years over the seriousness of low-level radiation and over how much danger there is from many years of exposure to it. There was little dispute over the dangers of over-exposure to high-energy radiation. The classic proof came from Marie Curie (1867–1934) and her husband, Pierre (1859–1906), who were early investigators of radioactivity. In his experiments, Pierre Curie deliberately exposed a patch of his skin to radiation and received a severe and slow-healing burn. His wife, who discovered radium, and their daughter Irène Joliot-Curie both died of leukemia, almost certainly as a result of years of exposure to radioactive materials.

But low levels of radiation are another matter. As with chemicals that accumulate in the environment, there are so-called safe limits for exposure to various radioactive elements. But no one can be really sure that people are safe even at the lower levels. For example, while alpha rays are so weak they hardly penetrate the skin, they can be dangerous if they are inhaled or swallowed and carried to vital organs. The long-term effects of radiation on us and our descendents as we are exposed to more and more of it is also unclear.

Again, we cannot ignore what radiation can do. We use it to kill diseased cells in our bodies, but it can damage healthy cells as well. It can also mutate, or change, our cells so that neither they nor their descendents can function normally. Here's how one physicist has explained the effects of radiation:

A small radiation dose may affect growing tissue and prevent a small proportion of the cells of those tissues from dividing. The remaining, unaffected cells take up the slack, however, and if the proportion of affected cells is small enough, symptoms never become visible.

In the genetic effect, however, there is no undamaged cell that can take over the work of the affected sex cell once fertilization has taken place. Suppose only one sex cell out of a million is damaged, then it will take part, on the average, in one out of every million fertilizations. And when it is used, it will not matter that there are 999,999 perfectly good sex cells that might have been used — it was the damaged cell that was used. That is why there is no . . . "safe" amount of radiation insofar as genetic effects are concerned. However small the quantity of radiation absorbed, mankind must be prepared to pay the price in a corresponding increase in the genetic load (the weight of undesirable genes that each species possesses).[3]

Whenever we discuss radiation, it is still the nuclear power plants that give us the most cause for concern. With their distinctive domes and towers, they have become almost as familiar on our landscapes as high-rise office buildings, fast-food chains, and gas stations.

Each one contains a reactor, a device that smashes large atoms to bits and in the process releases heat. Most reactors are built to produce electricity for commercial use. Others power submarines and ships and produce material for nuclear weapons. In a reactor that is used to generate electricity, the process is somewhat like what goes on inside any other electricity-producing plant that burns coal or oil. The big difference is that instead of coal and oil, the fuel used to drive reactors is generally uranium that is packed in long metal rods. The nuclei of the uranium are split apart by the same process that was used to make the atomic bomb, what the scientists call fission. As the nuclei burst, they release enormous amounts of heat; the heat vaporizes water to make steam, and the steam turns the blades of a turbine, which in turn drives the generator, which produces electricity. Uranium is a fantastic fuel because it produces many thousands of times more energy than can be generated by burning coal or oil. Just one ounce of uranium-235 gives off the same amount of energy as 388.4 barrels of oil!

But because a reactor's fuel is radioactive, and because so much heat and gamma rays are generated, reactors have to be shielded behind thick walls and cooled by constantly circulating water. Are reactors safe? Well, yes and no. Ordinarily, the harmful emissions are blocked and pose little danger to people working in a power plant or who live nearby. Nuclear power plants have strict operation regulations and all sorts of backup systems to guard against accidental discharge of injurious radiation. But accidents do happen on occasion. Operators make mistakes, and there may be mechanical failures within the reactor. And when a big mistake occurs in a nuclear power plant — as at Chernobyl and Three Mile Island — the world hears about it. The awful consequences of a Chernobyl are perhaps best expressed in the words of Dr. Valentin Belokon', the only physician who was on duty at the Chernobyl plant when the accident occurred. Dr. Belokon' was hospitalized the day after the accident with severe lung disease and remained in treatment for five months. Though he eventually returned to work, he suffered permanent breathing problems. Here is how he described the scene at Chernobyl:

> Three people came to me immediately. . . . They brought a chap of about eighteen. He was complaining of nausea and severe headache and had been vomiting. I took his blood pressure. It was a little high. Then it leapt up, and the chap became peculiar. Somehow not himself. . . . He became delirious before my very eyes. . . . He showed symptoms of confusion, couldn't speak and began to mumble as if he'd had a drink or two, although he didn't smell of alcohol. He was very pale. People who ran from the building kept exclaiming, "How awful." Then the chaps said that the dosimeters [devices worn by plant workers to register the amount of radiation to which they have been exposed] were hitting the top of their scales. . . .
>
> At six o'clock I began to feel a tickling in my throat. My head hurt. Did I understand the danger? Was I afraid? I understood. I was afraid. But when people see someone in a white coat nearby, it calms them. Like everyone else, I had no respirator, no protective clothing. Where was I to get a respirator? I would

have grabbed one. But there wasn't any. I telephoned the medical station in town. "Do we have any respirators?" "No, we don't." So that was that. Work in an ordinary gauze mask? It wouldn't have helped.[4]

Thankfully, scenes such as that one are not commonplace. But the fact that they can occur raises questions about the use of nuclear power for peaceful purposes. Should we close up all the nuclear plants? The United States has 111 nuclear plants in operation. How do we replace those and provide enough electricity for the people who now depend on the reactors? Should we rely on coal and oil for our electricity? We do have a lot of coal in the U.S., the equivalent of one trillion barrels of it, the same amount we'd find in 200 supergiant oil fields. At today's rate of consumption, we have enough coal to take us well into the twenty-fourth century. And with the proper safeguards when it is burned, it can be made relatively safe. But nuclear power is far more nonpolluting than both oil and coal, even when coal is made clean. Is that enough reason to continue to rely on nuclear power — and indeed expand its use — because coal and oil are going to run out someday? Can we build really safe reactors?

Again, hard questions to answer. Nuclear power is most efficient when everything is going right. New reactors, called breeders, actually produce more fuel than they use; that is, they make their own fuel by converting atomic material that is not readily split and able to release energy into material that is. Also, engineers are designing underground reactors, which are more efficient, safer, and far smaller than those now in use. These reactors require very small amounts of nuclear fuel packed not in large rods but in tiny ceramic balls so resistant to heat that they will not melt down.

There is also fusion. Fusion is different from fission. Fission breaks the nuclei of heavy, large atoms into smaller ones to produce energy. Fusion — which is the same awesome process that powers the sun, the stars, and the hydrogen bomb — takes place when the nuclei of small, light atoms are squeezed together, or fused, under fiery heat to form larger, heavier nuclei. This reaction produces huge amounts of energy, which, if it could be controlled and made to last, could give us an almost limitless supply of power. All we would need would be seawater, which contains the necessary elements that can be easily extracted. Just a tiny amount of one of those elements, deuterium, can produce the energy equivalent of 300 gallons of gasoline.

There are many advantages to fusion. Its fuel, seawater, is abundant and cheap. There is far less radioactivity associated with it than with fission. There is far less waste, and what there is would break down in a few hundred years, not the thousands it takes some other radioactive waste. And because so little fuel is required, a nuclear explosion is virtually impossible.

But fusion is not yet an option. Scientists are not yet able to control a fusion reaction. (The hydrogen bomb is powered by a fusion reaction, but it is an uncontrolled one.) To handle the heat generated in a fusion reaction would require reactors sturdy enough to withstand heat several times that of the sun. So far, scientists have been unable to build such a reactor.

So, we are left with fission reactors. And no matter what is done to improve them, they — at least at the current level of technology — will generate waste. And some nuclear waste is potentially far more dangerous and more difficult to dispose of than all the other ordinary garbage the world creates.

NUCLEAR WASTE

There are two kinds of nuclear waste. There is low-level radioactive waste, which contains small amounts of radioactivity. This sort of waste usually comes from medical facilities and pharmaceutical companies and includes clothing, test tubes, and all kinds of diagnostic trash. The other kind is high-level radioactive waste, which is created when fuel is mined and processed for reactors and when atoms are smashed. Such "hot" trash includes spent uranium fuel rods and the liquid waste produced when those rods are dissolved in acid to make plutonium for nuclear weapons.

Disposing of low-level radioactive waste presents difficulties but not insurmountable ones. It is shipped to special disposal sites in the United States. The public, however, is not always happy about radioactive waste — any radioactive waste — in its own backyards.

Because the very word *radioactivity* raises such fear in many individuals, stern regulations about the transportation and disposal of low-level radioactive waste are continually called for. Unfortunately, too often the public's concern is blown out of proportion and low-level radioactive waste is equated with the far more dangerous, and not easily disposed of, high-level radioactive waste that results from the nuclear fuel cycle. We cannot always blame the public for this because quite often public policy makers, long on political savvy but short on scientific knowledge, have neglected to get all the necessary facts about low-level radioactive waste and how it differs from the more dangerous forms. Without good information, the public will always fear anything remotely connected with nuclear power and will continue in extreme cases to equate what goes on in an X-ray laboratory with a plutonium bomb.

Of far more concern is how to dispose of our high-level radioactive waste. This problem has plagued us ever since the dawn of the nuclear age, and solutions have ranged from sending it into outer space to burying it under the ice in Antarctica. The U.S. alone has generated thousands of tons of "hot" waste, along with enough spent fuel to cover a football field to a height of three feet. It contaminates the earth, the water, and the air, and even specks of some of it can be extremely poisonous to humans. "The fact that every year there is enough waste being produced that will take the next three ice ages and beyond to become harmless," said Sir Crispin Tickell, British permanent representative to the United Nations, "is something that has deeply impressed the imagination."[5]

That assessment is a rightfully gloomy one. Short of abolishing nuclear energy altogether, it does seem that there is little we can do about our mounting accumulation of nuclear debris. Scientists are doing the best they can to cope with the problem, although admittedly the solutions are not long-term ones. There's a good chance that scientists will be able to build something that will contain nuclear waste for a few hundred years, but no one can even begin to think about building a storage facility that could contain nuclear waste for much more than that — such as a container that would safely hold plutonium, which remains dangerous for 240,000 years.

At the moment, high-level nuclear waste is stored near the reactors and weapons plants that manufacture it. Spent fuel rods are generally kept in pools of cold circulating water and the liquid waste in steel tanks that are buried below the ground. Some of the less radioactive liquid waste is mixed with concrete and made into blocks, which are buried just under the surface of the earth, under clay, and planted over. Other waste is being mixed with molten glass to be buried underground. Sometimes, waste has been dumped in the sea, encased in metal drums lined with concrete, other times just dumped as liquid without being packaged. In some countries, nuclear waste is recycled — that is, it is treated to recover plutonium, which can be used to fuel reactors.

Each of these methods has its drawbacks. Drums have leaked and contaminated surrounding land. Storing fuel rods in pools is only a temporary measure, and the pumps and filters required can malfunction. Earthquakes, volcanic eruptions, even the impact of a giant meteor (unlikely as it may be), can loosen the earth around buried nuclear waste, damage the drums and split the concrete and glass, and release radioactive material into the soil and groundwater. If a natural disaster doesn't free nuclear waste, the effect of naturally occurring groundwater — which saturates rocks everywhere under the ground — might do so. As the water flows through the rock, it could very well corrode the steel tanks that contain the nuclear waste, which would then mix with groundwater and leach out into the soil or streams. Recycling waste for plutonium is also not a simple solution. The process is costly and complex and still leaves some waste behind that must be disposed of. Worse is the fact that making plutonium from waste could lead to trade in the element, which can be used to make nuclear weapons as well as to generate electricity. If uranium is shipped overseas by a country for reprocessing into plutonium and the plutonium is returned to the home port, there is always the chance that the cargo could be hijacked by terrorists. Japan, for example, planned to have its uranium converted to plutonium overseas, then have the plutonium shipped back — 150 tons of it — for use as fresh fuel for the country's nuclear reactors.[6]

When all the options are considered, it would seem that the best way to permanently dispose of nuclear waste is, despite the potential danger, to bury it deep beneath the earth in some area that is very dry, isolated, and not apt to be vulnerable to natural disasters such as earthquakes and volcanic eruptions. But finding such a place is not as easy as it sounds. At this writing, the federal government was considering Nevada's Yucca Mountain as the primary site for a permanent nuclear waste dump because preliminary studies indicated that groundwater was unlikely to flood a repository if it were sunk 450 feet underground in a maze of tunnels more than 100 miles long. Some scientists are uncertain of that, however, and argue that groundwater even that far below the earth's surface would eventually seep up, perhaps forced upward by an earthquake. If all the opposition to the facility was put to rest, the dump would be ready to accept nuclear waste in the year 2010.

Is burying nuclear waste an invitation to disaster? Should we just leave it in barrels and pools on top of the ground and let it decay by itself, no matter how slowly that is, until we learn more about how to dispose of it safely or find new uses for it? Would you want it in your backyard? Again, not easy to answer. But one thing is certain. Nuclear waste must eventually be disposed of somewhere. And if we do not dispose of it now, your grandchildren, and their grandchildren, will have to deal with it, and at the current pace at which nuclear waste is being generated, that will be an even more formidable task than it already is. All we can hope for is that we will learn more about how radioactive elements behave, enough to allow us to solve this most pressing environmental problem.

7
THE PROBLEM:

TOO MUCH HEAT

Everybody talks about the weather," goes the familiar lament, "but nobody does anything about it." That means that we cannot control the weather. We cannot make rain or bring out the sun at the touch of a button, nor stop the frost from coming too soon, nor conjure up snow for Christmas, nor order a storm so we can have a day off from school.

We may not be able to do those things, but if some scientists are correct, we can do, and are doing, something else about the weather, something not so good: we can change the climate and make the whole earth heat up, with disastrous consequences.

Scientists call the temperature change global warming and the process that causes it the greenhouse effect. Together, along with the thinning of our ozone shield, they represent perhaps the worst of all the environmental disasters mentioned in this book. They are serious because they can affect the entire world, not just a part of it as occurs when we destroy a rain forest, spill oil in the ocean, or pollute the air over a city. Environmental assaults are quite often confined to one particular place and, as we have seen, they can often be dealt with, even reversed. In the case of weather, we are dealing with massive systems of invisible, moving air, with complicated temperature and pressure changes, all of which affects, directly or indirectly, everything that lives on earth. And if the upper atmosphere, where weather begins, is drastically altered, the situation is likely to remain unchanged for centuries, if not forever.

What is the greenhouse effect? The answer lies in those familiar glass-enclosed structures in which we cultivate and protect plants. The sun's rays stream through the glass of a greenhouse, but the glass also prevents the sun's heat from escaping and thus creates a warm, moist environment, just right for growing plants. According to scientists, the earth works under a similar system. But instead of glass, the earth is protected by so-called greenhouse gases — carbon dioxide, CFCs, nitrogen oxide, and methane. The greenhouse gases are transparent to the sun's rays; they let the rays in, just as glass does. The gases also trap heat very efficiently and keep it from escaping into outer space. The more greenhouse gases in the air, the more heat is trapped, and the warmer the earth gets.

When the greenhouse effect is working according to nature's plan, all is right with life on earth, just as in the glass-enclosed greenhouse. Without the heat-trapping ability of proper amounts of natural carbon dioxide in the air, our earth would be a frigid place all the time, with temperatures hovering on average around zero degrees Fahrenheit instead of the high fifties.

But over the years, we have added to the naturally occurring carbon dioxide in the air and also poured other gases into the atmosphere. The extra carbon dioxide comes from the burning of wood, coal, and oil. CFCs come from spray cans, nitrogen oxides from smokestacks and tailpipes, methane from natural gas and rotting garbage. Combined, these greenhouse gases are to blame for increasing the greenhouse effect that some scientists say could endanger Earth's climate one day.

Before we go on, let's acknowledge that not all scientists agree that global warming is the environmental threat that it has been made out to be. The ones who disagree say the greenhouse threat has been exaggerated, that too many scientists and environmentalists have a doom-and-gloom view of the world that is not backed up by the facts. Others go so far as to say that global warming, if it comes, will actually be good for the environment. Still other scientists, those who do not hold one view or the other, believe that the greenhouse theory makes sense but that the evidence is very thin.

Let's look first at the case for the greenhouse effect and for the notion that the world will experience a substantial warming, and let's consider what that would mean for us all. First of all, we know that the earth has experienced shifts in climate over the centuries. One piece of evidence for this is the Ice Ages, periods when massive glaciers covered large areas of the earth not ordinarily covered with ice. There have been several Ice Ages, and during the Ice Ages themselves or in between them, periods of warming are believed to have occurred. At the end of the last Ice Age, around 10,000 to 15,000 years ago, the temperature warmed by about nine or ten degrees Fahrenheit, and this warming apparently moved the Atlantic Ocean inland by a hundred miles. (Ocean water expands as it warms up, resulting in a rise in the sea level that covers beaches and other low-lying shoreline areas.) After that, the earth started to cool again, apparently moving toward another Ice Age.

Scientists are unsure whether the earth is now between Ice Ages or in a warm period between glaciers. But they believe that the earth's temperature has warmed up about one degree Fahrenheit over the last one hundred years — and that the warming is due to the gases that we have been putting into atmosphere. (According to climatologists, in 1990 the earth was the warmest it has been in any year since people began taking temperatures.) No one can say for sure that the temperature rise is due to natural variations or to the greenhouse effect, but there are some signs that the greenhouse effect is the cause. Glaciologists have drilled deep down into the ice of Antarctica and the Arctic and extracted cores of ancient ice. When they examined the cores, they found that the variations in the amount of carbon dioxide encased in the old ice corresponded with variations in temperatures over many thousands of years. The planetary warming effect of carbon dioxide may also be seen on other planets: Mars has very little carbon dioxide in its atmosphere and a temperature that never gets much warmer than around $-24°$ F; Venus, with plenty of carbon dioxide, has a fiery surface temperature of 850° F.[1]

We are not putting as much carbon dioxide into the atmosphere as Venus does, but we are putting more up there than ever before.

Two hundred or so years ago, the increases and decreases in the gas around the earth were the result of natural forces. As our industries and homes began burning more coal, oil, gas, and wood, carbon dioxide started pouring out far faster than plants and the oceans could absorb it. Between 1950 and 1980, worldwide emissions of carbon dioxide more than tripled, from 1.6 billion tons to 5.1 billion. About a quarter of all that gas is produced by the burning of fossil fuels in the United States; the generation of electricity in our country accounts for about 7.5 percent of the total worldwide emissions.[2] Deforestation, too, as we will see, is another important reason carbon dioxide builds up. When forests are burned or simply left to rot, they release the gas — and, of course, with no trees left standing less gas is absorbed and it flows into the atmosphere. One estimate is that the destruction of tropical rain forests — at the rate of 40,000 square miles a year — adds up to 1.6 billion tons of carbon dioxide to the atmosphere annually.[3]

What of the other greenhouse gases? Scientists know that they are also building up. And they undoubtedly will continue to do so, even though we might cut back on some of the activities that create the emissions. Too many countries, too many people, too many activities, are playing a part in the buildup for there to be any immediate halt in the process that leads to the greenhouse effect.

And it is not only burning trees or fossil fuels or running our cars and factories at full blast that are to blame. Other activities and processes contribute to the greenhouse problem. Consider cattle raising. The number of cattle in the world has doubled in the last forty years, and there is roughly one head of cattle for every four human beings. When all those cattle eat, bacteria break down the fiber in their guts into large quantities of methane gas — which is expelled in what we popularly refer to as farts. According to one estimate, the world's cattle send 100 million tons of methane into the atmosphere every year, enough to warm up the planet.[4]

Methane also comes from other sources: the muck from swamps and landfills, rice plants, which capture methane from the muddy bottoms of rice paddies, and even leaking gas mains. And do not think that methane is not as serious as carbon dioxide: in truth, it is far more powerful than carbon dioxide since it is able to trap twenty-five times as much of the sun's heat.

Okay, so greenhouse gases can trap heat and warm up the planet. But is it all that serious?

There are all sorts of grim scenarios about what would happen in a greenhouse world, most of them revolving around the melting of the polar ice caps. When that happens, the level of the world's oceans would rise enough to swamp low-lying areas. A swelling of the seas of just a foot would drown the Gulf and Atlantic coasts of the United States, and a three-foot rise would flood a sizable piece of Egypt, completely sink Venice, Italy, a city that is already waterlogged, and reduce London to a swamp. In the greenhouse world, global agricultural patterns would change drastically, vast ecosystems would be destroyed, plant life would grow out of control, sand dunes would disappear under water in flooded areas, sand would take over in areas dried by the increased heat, sea creatures that had been confined to one area of the world would suddenly appear in regions where they are unwanted, the warm weather would force more people outdoors and expose them to the sun's harmful rays, whole countries would be abandoned, forest fires would erupt without benefit of a match, tornadoes and hurricanes would be more common, and tropical diseases would find new places to establish a foothold.

As the World Health Organization observed during World Health Day in 1990:

> Global warming and the depletion of the ozone layer could prove to be calamities of the worst kind ever to have visited the Earth in the course of recorded history. . . . It is an Apocalyptical vision, but one that is of mankind's own making, unlike whatever cataclysm it was that caused the dinosaurs to vanish. The bad news is that, in one form or another, global climate change is coming. The good news is that we know about it and can and must benefit from that knowledge. Every little effort helps![5]

The Worldwatch Institute has also issued ominous warnings about global warming. Writing in the institute's report, *State of the World, 1990,* senior researcher Christopher Flavin notes:

> As the scientific evidence mounts, the time has arrived for a global warming agreement — comprehensive, detailed, and prescriptive. Only a rapid turnaround in carbon emissions trends can begin to get the world on the path to a stable climate. Wholesale changes in energy, land use, and population policies are implied. Unless such action is taken in the next few years, however, the nineties will become a lost decade for the world's atmosphere, relegating the next generation to a world less able to meet growing human needs. No other environmental problem has such an exponential and cumulative dimension to it, a fact that argues persuasively for the immediate adoption of strong policies.[6]

Strong words, those. But will it happen? If so, when?

The scientists who believe that the greenhouse world is coming say that the earth will definitely warm by three to eight degrees Fahrenheit within the next sixty or so years. They argue that even the single degree the earth has already warmed in the last century is enough to cause changes in the way glaciers behave.

Not all scientists feel the same way, however. Some argue that not enough is known yet about the behavior of climate to make dire predictions, that the tiny temperature rise already noted in the last hundred years has not been definitely tied to greenhouse gases, and that other factors — among them less use of CFCs and lessened activity in the sun in the next century — will delay, or offset, any major climate changes. Some scientists are even stronger in their opinions. They call the research that points to a global warming disaster "junk science." And they argue that even if the predicted warming trend comes on schedule, it will not cause the massive destruction the doomsayers predict. Rather, the worst that might happen is that some cities would sustain some flooding, but no worse than what Holland and Venice and other low-lying areas have had to deal with for centuries.

Among those who have argued that the effects of greenhouse

warming have been exaggerated is Dixy Lee Ray, former governor of the state of Washington and former chairwoman of the U.S. Atomic Energy Commission. "Why do so many people believe in the dire forecasts?" she has asked. And she continues:

> Perhaps the historian Hans Morgenthau was right when he wrote in 1946: "The intellectual and moral history of mankind is the story of insecurity, of the anticipation of impending doom." John Maddox, editor of the British journal, *Nature*, says, "But these days there also seems to be an underlying cataclysmic sense among people. Scientists don't seem to be immune to this." Well, they ought to be. What the greenhouse debate needs most is a dose of healthy skepticism.[7]

Meteorology professor Richard Lindzen of the Massachusetts Institute of Technology is another prominent skeptic. He has said that the greenhouse effect "is the only subject in atmospheric science where a consensus view has been declared before the research has hardly begun."[7]

Other scientists have been arguing that even if too much carbon dioxide gets into the air and the earth's climate does warm up a bit, the effect might be good for us. More carbon dioxide in the air, they say, would mean more plants and increased harvests, even plants growing in places that had been too dry to support growth. More plants would mean less soil erosion, and more organic matter being returned to the soil to make it more fertile. "Botanists and other plant scientists refer to the rising carbon dioxide content of the earth's atmosphere as atmospheric carbon dioxide enrichment and aerial carbon dioxide fertilization," said one scientist in a recent letter to the *New York Times*. "It's one of the best things that could happen to the planet. So let's tell both sides. The facts demand it. Reason dictates it. Earth deserves it."[8]

SOME SOLUTIONS

If the people who believe in the greenhouse effect are correct, we had better do something about it fast. If the skeptics are correct, the forecasts of global warming and its causes are too uncertain to hang public policy on or to force any drastic change in our habits.

Given the difference of opinion, what do we do? Do we take steps to halt a problem that may not occur?

The best wisdom says it is better to be safe than sorry, that if we are going to err it is better to err on the side of some sort of action, action that, like mother's chicken soup, cannot harm us and might, indeed, do us some good. But what kind of action?

For one thing, the new Clean Air Act may help by forcing us to cut down on some of what we put into the air. Next, since carbon dioxide seems to be half the problem, it is obvious that global emissions of this gas should be reduced. That, unfortunately, is easier said than done. For the world to make a significant reduction in carbon dioxide, there would have to be a drastic cutback in our reliance on fossil fuels and a halt to deforestation — both complicated solutions. Efforts to curb carbon dioxide emissions had bogged down in the United States at this writing, although a few other countries are planning to reduce them.

Realistically, we cannot just ban carbon dioxide outright as we banned CFCs, but we can take steps to reduce its presence. Taxes could be imposed on all fossil fuels, and rebates could be given to fuel companies that plant trees. We could burn more methane gas, both to obtain energy from it and to get rid of it. There are other schemes, some of them requiring tinkering with the environment itself. For instance, scientists are looking into the possibility of growing tons of seaweed and other plant life, and spreading it all over the oceans so it could absorb carbon dioxide from the air. That might work, but then again it might not: all the extra plant life might upset the balance of nature and do irreparable damage to the environment.

In the last analysis, the most feasible plan is to cut emissions. To do that requires conservation of energy and increased use of clean, renewable energy sources. This does not mean we should abolish the use of coal, oil, and gas. Despite the bad press these fuels have gotten lately, the fossil fuels do not have to be the bad guys. Yes, they create damage to the environment because of the haphazard way they are currently burned. But they, along with nuclear fuel, are also incredibly valuable to the world and, for the moment at least, still the best energy sources we have. They should continue to be used, but with proper controls and modifications, along with alternative sources of energy. Perhaps only then will we really be able to do something about the weather.

The key to the greenhouse effect — and indeed to virtually every one of the environmental problems we have been discussing — appears to be practicing something that also helps every one of us live a happier, healthier life: moderation.

8
THE PROBLEM:

DEFORESTATION

What do we plant when we plant the tree?
We plant the ship that will cross the sea,
We plant the mast to carry the sails,
We plant the planks to withstand the gales —
The keel, the keelson, and beam and knee —
We plant the ship when we plant the tree.
                                        — Henry Abbey

True enough, those words. But trees provide us with far more than ships. Trees have also given shelter to countless generations of people, animals, and plants. And for us humans, even more than that. Trees have given us four-poster beds and telephone poles, floorboards and fuel, fruits and nuts, vanilla and maple syrup, rubber and alcohol, pulp for paper and turpentine for our painting chores. Even when they have been dead for a long time trees have given us another valuable resource: coal from their decayed remains. Trees also play a most important role in protecting the world's climate by absorbing the carbon dioxide exhaled by all animals, an excess of which contributes to the greenhouse effect.

No wonder that there is another, more familiar, poem about trees. Written by G. P. Morris, it offers some stern advice:

Woodman, spare that tree!
Touch not a single bough!
In youth it sheltered me,
And I'll protect it now.

Sadly, many people do not spare the trees or protect them. Some of us forget that Native Americans and other primitive peoples worshipped trees for the things they give us and prayed to gods that were said to dwell in them. We sometimes take advantage of the trees' generosity. We take from them to satisfy our real needs, it is true, and that is acceptable. But we also plunder them and treat them badly in other ways. We overcut our forests because the lumber business is profitable. Trees are chopped down to give poor people land for farming and ranching, because rich landowners prefer that to giving the poor access to better land that is already productive and profitable. Trees that should not be cut down fall indiscriminately when loggers run roughshod through the forests with their heavy equipment. We clear out huge tracts of forestland and ruin wildlife habitats to make room for new cities, and we forget that we need to replace what we have removed. Forests are destroyed for fuel by people whose impoverished living conditions require it but who might not have to take such measures if we improved their way of life. And there is carelessness, a discarded cigarette that burns millions of acres of forest along with the fragile ecosystems that give them their unique forms of life. There is even occasional malice: in Texas recently, a man was sent to prison for nine years for poisoning a 500-year-old oak.

Once upon a time, before the development of agriculture, forests covered 12 to 16 billion acres of the world. Perhaps half of that amount remains today.[1] As forests are hacked down and burned and cleared away, all that is left in many parts of the world are barren tracts of land that look like moonscapes or are but soggy muck in which little can grow or live.

Especially endangered are the tropical rain forests with their population of exotic life-forms. These dense jungles cover about seven percent of the world's surface and are among our most vital resources. They are creations of breathtaking beauty, part of an ancient, 3,000-mile wide belt of lush greenery that girdles the equatorial regions of the earth — Brazil, central Africa, Southeast Asia, and Indonesia — and touches other tropical regions such as Hawaii, the Virgin Islands, and Puerto Rico. Rain forests are also the home of millions of species of organisms — plants, animals, and microorganisms. Jaguars and parrots, pythons and orchids, and precious mahogany and rubber trees all thrive in the rain forests. The forests regulate water flow by trapping rain for farmers, who grow food for over one billion people; they also help prevent floods and soil erosion. Rain forests control the climate, not only for people who live in or near them but for the rest of the world.

But they are being destroyed, and faster than any other natural habitat. Every year, more than 35 million acres of tropical forest — an area roughly the size of the state of Florida — are wiped out by commercial logging, by agricultural expansion to provide croplands for growing populations and land for cattle ranching, by road building, the building of new hydroelectric dams and plantations, and the increasing demand for fuel. When the trees fall, sunlight that is harmful to many life-forms is let in, and at least one species of plant, animal, or insect is made extinct every day. "Within the next thirty years," observed biologist Peter Raven in 1986,

> all of the tropical forests will have been eliminated, with the exception of a few remnants on places too steep or too wet to cultivate. The major priority is the problem of extinction. The reduction of biodiversity is worldwide. Our boat is sinking, and we don't even act like we know it.[2]

Two years after those comments, however, much of the world did become more aware of the rain forests. Unfortunately, it took a murder in Brazil to do it. The victim was Francisco (Chico) Mendes, a worker who made a living in the Amazon jungle gathering latex, the milky substance in wild trees from which rubber is made. But Mendes was no ordinary rubber tapper. As the leader of a union of thousands of rubber tappers, he became an outspoken critic of the ranchers and developers who were destroying the Brazilian rain forests. For fifteen years, Mendes had been angering ranchers and others for demanding that the government set aside large areas of rain forest where workers and their families would be allowed to harvest rubber and nuts without having to worry that the forests would be burned down by developers. Several attempts were made on his life, and he received many death threats. A few days before Christmas in 1988, Mendes was killed by a shotgun blast in the backyard of his home. Eventually, a rancher and his son were convicted of the murder, and Mendes became the first martyr for an environmental cause and an international symbol of the battle to protect the Brazilian rain forests.

And it is Brazil's rain forests that seem to be bearing the brunt of the devastation. In six Amazonian states, the deforested area increased by more than 150 percent between 1975 and 1978; since then, nearly 12 percent of the Amazon area, which is two-thirds the size of the United States, has been chopped down or burned. In one of those states, Rondonia, 20 percent or more of the forests are now completely gone, forests that made up some of the most beautiful rain forests in the world. Rondonia's problems began decades ago when thousands of poor urban workers were encouraged by the government to go to the state, where they would be given free land after clearing out the rain forests to build roads and establish farms and towns. But after the forests were cleared away, the workers found that the land was not suitable for growing crops (the rainfall in the forests washes away all the nutrients in the soil), and many of the workers, most of them poor Indians, were left with only meager means of support. Thousands of them have died from disease and violence because of what many people believe to be ill-conceived development projects that have also killed a precious ecosystem and the wide variety of life-forms in it.

The rain forests are generally destroyed by slashing and burning, with burning the easiest and most inexpensive way to do the job. But so many fires have been set in Brazil that not only are the workers affected, but the smoke has been spotted as far away as Antarctica! At one time, the smoke over Rondonia and other states was so thick that airports had to be closed for days. Photographs of Brazil taken by the space shuttle Discovery revealed a vast cloud of smoke large enough to cover most of India.[3]

While Brazil stands as the worst example of rain forest destruction, other areas of the world are watching their rain forests disappear, too. Indonesia is one such place. Formerly known as the Netherlands East Indies, Indonesia is a country in Southeast Asia that is made up of Java, Sumatra, part of Borneo, and many other smaller islands. One of the islands, Java, had some of the greenest rain forests on earth, but they, too, have dwindled to well below what is considered an ecologically safe limit — 30 percent forest — because of the need for fuel and cropland. Moreover, because so much of the forest cover has disappeared from Java, every time it rains — which occurs often and in huge downfalls — heavy flooding results. The floods ruin the soil and any crops that have been planted. It is not unusual on Java for floodwaters to wash millions of cubic feet of soil into the sea in a single rainy season. To keep up with the island's food needs, more and more rain forest has to be cut down to make room for cropland — cropland that was never all that productive to begin with.

Hawaii has also seen its rain forests destroyed. The isolated state is a unique place that deserves our attention for many reasons, one of which is the fact that 95 percent of its flowering plants and 99 percent of its animal life are found only there. Too many people do not seem to care about that, however. The islands that make up Hawaii have been deforested for many years, and more than 60 percent of the rain forests have been torn away to make room for plantations, ranches, and city buildings. Trees are also downed so that they can be ground into wood chips and burned by power plants to produce electricity. With the destruction, many species of plants and animals have been wiped out. According to one account a few years ago, Hawaii's forests once supported fifty-seven species of birds, but twenty-three were extinct and twenty-three more were endangered. Only eleven were considered safe.[4]

When one considers that rain forest land is not suitable for agriculture — nor for cattle raising for very long, either — and that there are other ways to generate electricity besides burning precious trees, it is difficult to fault those who would preserve these forests at all costs. None of the actions that destroy rain forests seem to make any sense, except to those who see only a short-term profit. Apart from the destruction of the trees and the threat to the ecology, there is the damage that is done to the people who live in and near the forests. We have seen what happened to the Indians who were lured to Rondonia, and the same sort of thing has happened to poor people elsewhere. Many times, Indians are forced to leave forests that have been their ancestral homes because of the destruction. Here's how Rainforest Action Network, a concerned group in San Francisco, has described a situation in West Papua, Indonesia:

> That is an area rich in oil, copper, nickel, cobalt, tin, silver, molybdenum and timber, within one of the largest rainforests on earth. Multi-national corporations are drooling with excitement. But it's also an area where 800,000 native people have lived for thousands of years. Now these people are being driven off their lands. More than 10,000 have already been killed for their resistance, and the land is being cleared and destroyed as fast as any on earth. Indonesia's Minister of Transmigration has put the case clearly: "The different ethnic groups of Indonesia will disappear . . . and there will be one kind of man." In other contexts, they call that genocide. Your tax dollars pay for it.[5]

All the attention that is paid to rain forests is warranted, of course, but sometimes it distracts us from thinking about the other kinds of forests that are being chopped down or burned away, sometimes indiscriminately. We need to cut down trees, of course, to obtain timber, a leading commodity. In the U.S., wood and wood products are big business, accounting for billions of dollars in sales and the employment of hundreds of thousands of people. Trees cover a third of the United States, and they supply us, and people in many other countries, with a variety of materials.

But how many trees to cut down and how to replace the ones we do cut are questions that often pit environmentalists against loggers. The timber industry, for example, wants to keep cutting down trees in the nation's old public forests in the Pacific Northwest, arguing that old growth will regenerate in time. Environmentalists feel that one cannot predict future growth accurately and that cutting down ancient forests will devastate the ecosystem and endanger important wildlife. They want strict limits placed on how many trees can be taken out of national forests and would like to see old-growth areas federally protected. Loggers in the U.S. do replant where they cut down, but sometimes not enough, according to some preservationists. Sometimes, too, the new trees that are planted are so similar to one another in size, shape, and kind, and stuck into the ground in such ordered fashion, that they look less like nature's handiwork and more like rows of bowling pins; the diversity and the casual appearance that once characterized the now cut-down forest and kept its multitude of life-forms in delicate balance are no more. On commercial tracts and in national forests, planting now keeps pace with harvest, and because of conservation programs, according to the American Forestry Association, there is no net loss of forestlands. But in the urban forests, the forests near and in cities that make up about 15 percent of our forests, it seems to be another story. As city limits expand, many trees are cut down, and we are losing more of them than we replant: for every four trees that die in the urban forest, only one is replanted.[6]

SOME SOLUTIONS

Can we save the world's forests? Yes, if there is cooperation between those who must remove some of them to supply the world's needs and make way for legitimate development and those who would protect them. You have probably read of radical groups of environmentalists who have driven spikes into trees to prevent loggers from cutting them down, and you probably know that sometimes banks finance environmentally destructive projects, among which are those that wipe out rain forests. Should people take drastic and sometimes dangerous measures to stop loggers? Should world lenders be stopped from financing development projects if it means ruining a valuable ecosystem? Is it more important to harvest ancient trees for the wood they provide us with or to protect the spotted owls that live in their branches? Should the taking of ancient trees be prohibited altogether? Should we ban all development in and around rain forests?

It is unrealistic to believe that all logging can and should be stopped and that we will quit depending on wood and wood products. That is as simpleminded an argument as the one that says we can and should ban all motor vehicles to wipe out air pollution and that all of our energy needs can be met by turning to windmills and solar energy. Perhaps one day in the far distant future, humankind will come up with alternatives that allow us to preserve all of our natural resources 100 percent. You and I will certainly not see that day, nor does it appear that any of your grandchildren or their grandchildren will.

This doesn't mean that we shouldn't be careful about how much logging we do and where we do it. Both preservation and economic growth have to be considered in logging, as they must in many of the other potentially troublesome industries we have been considering throughout this book.

In the case of the rain forests, trees that are needed for the things they produce can be cut selectively and in limited numbers, leaving more standing than are chopped down. The more delicate areas of rain forests can also be protected by law, with only the sturdiest sections open to limited harvesting. Governments can try to make money from their rain forests without cutting them down — by organizing tours and safaris, using them for plant and animal research, tapping them for medicines and other products. Governments could crack down on moneylenders who fund development projects, denying them access to rain forests if they do not do all they can to protect them. If rain forests must be cut down, care should be taken to remove specimens that have exceptional value and transplant them to botanical gardens.

Finally, the problem of poverty and uneven land distribution in the regions where rain forests thrive should be addressed. People would not be so apt to rush to a rain forest and slash or burn it if they had better ways of making a living or if land were made available to them through land reform instead of promising them boggy rain forest land that is not suitable for agriculture or ranching. It has been said that 4 percent of Brazil's landowners own 80 percent of the farmland, far more than they need, while 70 percent of rural households are landless. Giving poor Indians inexpensive rain forest land may be far cheaper and easier than sharing some of the vast tracts of valuable land that are available, but it is not exactly fair.

Insofar as the rest of the world's forests are concerned, most have already been logged or cleared out. So we have to pay careful attention to how much wood we take from them and to reforesting. We could see to it, as in the rain forests, that timber is used up no faster than it can be replaced. We could at least temporarily halt the cutting of old-growth forests, giving nature time to regenerate the landscape, and we could plant more trees in urban areas and be a bit more careful about how many we take out every time we build a house or a gas station. We have to consider the nontimber side of forestry — the biodiversity, the roughshod methods that are often used to cut trees down, the environment-wrecking roads that loggers build — as well as the chief product of the forests, the timber itself.

Some loggers, at the urging of soil biologists and other researchers, are already practicing what is known as new forestry, a U.S. Forest Service program that tries to balance the needs of the loggers and the environmentalists. One exemplary program of this type is the planned Shasta Costa Valley Project in the Pacific Northwest, a tree-cutting/preservation program that aims to keep the valley ecologically healthy, with timber taking a secondary goal.

The project, as described by Worldwatch, allows only 1 percent of the valley's ancient forests to be cut, with no logging allowed on the 2,200 acres of low-elevation old-growth, the Northwest's oldest and most biologically valuable ecosystem. (A gram of soil in the area can contain 10,000 species of organisms.) Logging is concentrated in groups of trees less than 200 years old, and these are to be thinned, not cleared. The total amount of wood to be cut is a third less than earlier proposals by the Forest Service, which favored timber production.

Foresters in the Shasta Costa Valley would carefully select which trees would be logged and which would be left alone to help the land recover. Moreover, logging would be concentrated near existing roads on the valley's edges, and helicopters would be used to get the rest of the wood out — measures that would save the ground from being torn up and thus preserve the natural habitats of the various life-forms.[7] Whether any of these measures will help remains to be seen. But we must try.

9
THE PROBLEM:

THREATENED WILDLIFE

Wildlife is a broad term, but we use it here to refer to all nonhuman wild, living things — mammals, birds, fish, insects, reptiles, amphibians, and, of course, plants. The variety is enormous — far, far more diverse than that of any of the familiar creatures we might see in a Disney cartoon or in a geography book or a zoo. From armadillos to zebras, shipworms to Dungeness crabs, gnats to harlequin beetles, Amazonian buriti palms to the sagebrush of the American West, the list seems almost endless.

Scientists estimate that there are between 3 and 30 million species of life on earth and that more than half of them live in the tropical rain forests. While the number of life-forms is impressive, the number that has actually been identified and cataloged is not: less than two million.

But for all this variety among animals and plants, they do have one thing in common: no matter if they walk, crawl, fly, swim, or just grow quietly in the earth or in the water, they are vulnerable to our recklessness. Like the dinosaurs, wooly mammoths, and saber-toothed tigers, which disappeared long ago from the face of the earth, many of today's animals and plants may soon be gone forever. One day, they may be declared extinct, for they are an endangered species, the life-forms that human activities — overpopulation, pollution, roughshod agricultural and construction practices, introducing new species to established areas, overhunting of some animals for fur, feathers, and ivory — are slowly and surely wiping out. (The term *endangered* is generally applied to wildlife facing extinction, and the word *threatened* is often used to describe wildlife that is apt to become endangered in the near future.) Much of our wildlife will, of course, continue to thrive. Some of it will even overthrive: many of the animals and plants that proliferate will be the tougher pests, the unwanted weeds that take over a neglected garden, the rats that have overrun the places where more desirable species had once lived peacefully.

It is true that nature has a way of weeding itself out without any help from us. This has been the case ever since the beginning of evolution — the process by which living things change and adapt to their surroundings. It is also true that extinction is part of nature's plan: animals and plants sometimes become extinct as they compete with one another for space, the fittest ones, the ones with the right genetic character, surviving. Even forests are thinned out by nature. Struck regularly by lightning, they are set afire and burn, a terrible consequence when we think of the devastation created by forest fires set by humans, but which sometimes has a favorable outcome: fires eradicate disease that might ruin a whole species, they make room for stronger trees to thrive, and they even force some kinds of trees to set their seeds and grow new trees.

Such natural events as evolution and weather-caused forest fires do not generally run out of control to the extent that they kill animal and plant species in enormous numbers. Some scientists tell us that a gigantic comet or asteroid blasted the earth some 65 million years ago, killing all the plants. Deprived of their plant food, the theory goes on, the dinosaurs were all soon wiped out. Another recent theory says that the giant asteroid contained huge amounts of the metal nickel and that when it hit, it spread enough vaporized nickel around to poison all the plants that the dinosaurs fed on. Other scientists suggest that other ocean-blasting comets periodically killed off other forms of life during the earth's early days.

But, fortunately, such events have not occurred on the modern earth. There are plenty of plants and animals on the land and in the water. They reproduce, sometimes in very large numbers, as do fruit flies and rabbits — and they may produce far more offspring than necessary to keep the population at the size it ought to be. When we consider that there may be as many as 30 million different life-forms on earth — an abundance that scientists call biodiversity — and that each one seems to thrive and adapt very well to its surroundings, it is difficult to imagine any of them being killed off in numbers appreciable enough to make much of a difference, much less lead to extinction.

Without trying to paint a hopeless gloom-and-doom scenario, let's say that nature can be overwhelmed by human activities. We are quite capable of speeding up the rate by which some species decline, are made extinct, or in some cases run out of control. An example of the latter is the European starling. Brought to the United States from Europe in the late 1800s, it now has taken over the nesting sites of our native bluebirds and woodpeckers. Whether by accident, in the name of progress, or out of necessity, human beings are setting up a scenario that could make the earth an eerily quiet place one day in the distant future. According to Peter Raven, director of the Missouri Botanical Garden, humans will, over the next three decades, drive an average of 100 species to extinction every day. Indeed, scientists speculate that the present rate of extinction is at least 1,000 times the rate that has been the norm since prehistoric days.[1]

The key word here is *change*. When the environment changes and when the plants or animals that live in it have not acquired the traits required to adapt to it, they die out. Some plants and animals, including humans, can get used to certain shifts in living conditions, but only if they are exposed to the changes slowly. Mountain climbers, for instance, usually experience shortness of breath and rapid heartbeat when they go to high altitudes, where oxygen is in short supply. But after the climbers stay for a while in such an environment, they don't mind the altitude. They have acclimated.

Acclimation is not the same as adaptation. Acclimation is not handed down from generation to generation. The mountain climbers' children will not automatically be able to survive in the high altitude. On the other hand, offspring of fish and animals that live in the Arctic regions will be able to survive in the freezing temperature because both parents and offspring have adapted to the harsh conditions — and adaptation is handed down through the generations. The offspring have acquired, through heredity, the necessary characteristics that allow them to survive.

But while acclimation enables some plants and animals to live outside their normal habitats and adaptation allows life-forms to thrive in very harsh conditions, this does not mean that living things can live anywhere and under any conditions. Nature has imposed strict limits on all of us. Saltwater plants still cannot live in fresh water, nor could an Arctic fish live very long in your swimming pool. Nothing that we know of can exist on the sun, or, without a space suit, in the vacuum of space.

What humans have done, with all our oil spills and chemicals, our airborne pollutants, our acid rain and global warming, and our unrestrained land development, is to create a hostile environment for many animals and plants. When the Exxon *Valdez* spilled nearly 11 million gallons of crude oil off southeastern Alaska, the oil reportedly poisoned some 250,000 sea birds, killing thousands of them; the oil may also have destroyed nearly 10,000 sea otters, 150 bald eagles, at least a dozen whales and no one knows how many sea plants. And it is not only the familiar animals and plants, or the biggest ones, that are affected by careless human behavior. Fauna and flora (meaning animals and plants) you probably never heard of are also in danger: the lotus blue butterfly, the golden-headed tamarind, the birdwing pearly mussel, the western prairie fringed orchid, the Kauai Oo, the snail darter. The tiny plankton we discussed earlier, the algae that live in ponds, the mosses and ferns and insects hidden in the forests — all are affected by our destructive habits. Moreover, some of these uncommon life-forms have been reduced to only a dozen or so survivors.

Should we be concerned about tiny creatures that live at the bottom of a pond or at the base of a tree somewhere far away? We most certainly should. Nothing that lives is insignificant. Every plant and animal has been given life, as well as a unique characteristic that enables it to play a part in the whole ecosystem. Each living thing on earth, no matter how large or how small, is important because it has an effect on every other living thing in its community. We have seen how the food chain works, and there are many other examples of interdependency, of interrelationship. Some plants make a special home for a certain kind of animal or fish. Destroy the plants and you destroy the creature's habitat, and the creature. Every time you tear out a weed or turn over a rock, you force some living creature out into the hostile open. Bees pollinate plants and make honey with the nectar they pick up from flowers. Destroy the bees, or the plants, and you stop pollination and the manufacture of honey that is used to supply the beehive during the winter. Strip a plant of its leaves, and you may be depriving a grasshopper of its food, and if the grasshopper is wiped out, so is the food source for some birds. Chop down the trees in a wetlands area, and you destroy the habitat of mosquito-eating bats and birds, leaving the mosquitoes to plague us. Human beings, too, are part of this network. Without plants, which draw energy from the sun and turn it into food of all kinds, we would perish. Without plants, there would be no oxygen in the air for us to breathe.

There is a theory of the interrelationship of living things that views the whole earth as a living organism. First expressed by James Lovelock, a British scientist, the theory is known as Gaia. The word, pronounced GUY-uh, comes from the name of the Greek goddess of the earth. The Gaia theory suggests that all of the living organisms on this planet work together with rocks, air, gases, minerals, and water. This relationship between biological forms and nonbiological forms is seen as a self-regulating system that maintains a stable global environment for all life.

The Gaia theory is a controversial one. Scientists agree that plants and animals affect elements of the nonliving world, and a familiar example, of course, is photosynthesis. This is the process we mentioned in our discussion of dying water, the mechanism by which plants convert the energy from sunlight into chemical energy, which is then stored as carbohydrates. Photosynthesis also produces another essential nonliving material, oxygen, and indeed the majority of oxygen in the atmosphere is the product of photosynthesis. But the disagreement comes over whether the relationship between life and inanimate matter is as incredibly close as Gaia holds, and whether the whole system actually regulates itself.

But let's return to the interrelationships among living things. We said that each living thing has an effect on every other one in some given space. One example of the effects of such a tightly bound relationship may be seen in influenza, which we all know as the flu. Every major flu epidemic has begun in China, but not because of geography or climate. For many years, Chinese farmers have raised pigs and ducks together, and it is this close relationship between the two that produces new strains of flu virus. This is how it works. A flu virus passes from the ducks to the pigs. At the same time, a human flu virus also goes from the farmer to the pigs. The pigs now become "mixing vessels" for the two kinds of virus. Inside the pigs, the human and duck viruses exchange genes, and this reshuffling of heredity instructions creates a new flu virus — one that can infect humans and that might even be more dangerous than the original human virus. Because any human who is infected with this new flu virus has not built up any immunity to it, the disease spreads rapidly into an epidemic.

The duck-pig flu story is not only an example of the links between various creatures. It also demonstrates what can happen when some human activity — in the flu case, the mingling of pigs and ducks — dictates how certain animals live. For often when we disrupt an ecosystem, we create enormous problems for ourselves as well as for the displaced life-forms. Tearing up a patch of forest or a field or building a dam can give some viruses and other disease-carrying microorganisms new opportunities to spread. Global warming can change the migration pattern of animals or the habitats of rodents and insects, enabling them to carry viruses to other regions. Dams, irrigation systems, and hydroelectric power plants are necessary, but building them often creates large reservoirs, drainage ditches, and ponds. And more water means more bloodsucking mosquitoes — mosquitoes that carry disease.

Dr. Stephen Morse, a virologist at Rockefeller University in New York City, calls such movement viral traffic. As he has put it,

More often than not, what causes the emergence of these viruses and diseases is some human activity, some environmental or social change that promotes the transfer of viruses to new hosts.[2]

There are many recent examples of what scientists call emerging viruses, viruses that environmental changes help bring out of hiding or help move from a place where they have been prevalent to one where they have not. One is the virus that causes Argentine hemorrhagic fever, a severe bleeding disease. The virus is carried by a mouse that lives in cornfields. When Argentine farmers recently stopped their traditional practice of mixing crops and began clearing land so that they could plant only large crops of maize, they gave the little mouse a new and very large home. At the same time, herbicides dumped on the area to kill weeds changed the diversity of the other plant life and, as a result, the diversity of all the rodent species. Eventually, the mouse that carried the virus dominated.

There are numerous other examples of how the activities of human beings are affecting animals and plants. We've already seen how fertilizers dumped into the water cause the growth of suffocating blooms of algae and how wetland development can kill native grasses. But life-forms far larger than algae and grass are at peril in our waters. Just about every fish and marine mammal is beleaguered by human beings who overhunt it, pollute it with chemicals, or kill it accidentally while pleasure-boating or fishing.

Among the largest of the endangered creatures of the deep are whales, the marine animals that have been hunted for centuries for their meat, ivory, oil, bone, and (in the sperm whale) a precious waxy substance called ambergris that is used to make perfume. Some whales are incredibly huge, like the blue whale, the largest animal ever to have lived on Earth. Up to ninety feet long and weighing as much as 150 tons — far more than an elephant, the largest earthbound mammal — blue whales used to be plentiful but are now scarce because of overhunting, the human activity that puts them at special risk.

Whale hunting was once a widespread, accepted practice, and the United States was the world leader in whaling between 1820 and 1860, the peak years for taking whales. But what was once acceptable during a time when whale products were essential is now frowned on by many nations, including, ironically, the United States. Environmentalists want a total ban on whaling, arguing that it is going on far beyond today's human needs and is putting a whole class of mammals at risk of extinction.

Despite the calls for a ban, whale hunting for ivory and meat continues, primarily by Japan and the Soviet Union. The issue is a sticky one. The Japanese, especially, insist on being allowed to take whales. Generations of Japanese have been brought up on whale meat, and it has been included for years in school lunch programs. Japanese whalers say that they do not hunt whales recklessly, that their scientific studies show that whale stocks are not decreasing but increasing, and that because of the increase a certain amount of whaling is necessary to maintain a balance and preserve the whale's existence. If they do not hunt whales, say the Japanese, there will be too many whales for the available food, and their numbers will die out by natural selection.

Tempers can run high over the whaling issue. Here's how one Japanese writer once expressed his feelings about the critics of whaling:

> The sentimental view that the whale is a wonderfully clever and beautiful creature whose disappearance would be a pity is allowed to predominate. I see a glaring discrepancy in this kind of approach.
>
> Westerners employ a religious interpretation that condones the eating of pigs and cattle, since God created these animals for man's food, but considers it a sin to eat anything else. Accordingly, it is apparently wrong and cruel to eat whale meat.
>
> I simply cannot understand what is good about the anti-whaling movement nor why it is so hotly pursued. Childish arguments against whaling continue to build: the whale's cry is so pitiful, the whale's tiny eyes seem to be weeping tears of accusation, the whale is the most clever of animals after man, and the great, majestic whale is a living testimony of the evolution of animals.
>
> The Westerner's view of the Japanese as barbaric, and the whale as a creature to be pitied clearly stems from a life-view

based on meat-eating habits. The actual situation of the Japanese is completely ignored.

Any race considers its own reasoning to be absolute and right. . . . There are those who laugh at the Japanese for clinging to the whale when it only provides one percent of their protein. But the whale's history as a part of the Japanese diet is quite old — the whale is even mentioned in Japan's oldest anthology of poems. There is also a saying that one whale means wealth for seven villages — several villages benefited from just one whale.[3]

Despite that impassioned argument, there are restrictions on whaling, especially against the wholesale slaughter that was once common. Strict limits have been set on how many whales and what kind can be taken. Some whales, such as the gigantic blue whale and the humpback whale, are protected and may not be hunted legally. What are your thoughts about whaling? Does the Japanese writer make any valid points? Should the Japanese be allowed to continue whaling because it is a cultural tradition in their country? Is the fact that a whale is a mammal, like us, and intelligent, a reason for stopping its being used as a food source? Does killing whales justify providing only one percent of a country's food supply?

Another seagoing creature that is imperiled by human action is the dolphin. A dolphin is actually a small-toothed whale and is highly intelligent — some people contend that dolphins are as intelligent as humans. They are not aggressive, and indeed, as anyone knows who has watched them play in aquariums and theme parks, they are quite friendly. Dolphins are not generally hunted — that is, not deliberately. But they are caught accidentally by tuna fishermen when huge, circular nets are spread over the ocean. Dolphins school together with tuna in some waters, and fishermen look for dolphins when they're looking for tuna. When the nets are dropped to catch the fish, the dolphins are also caught inside. The trapped dolphins die fairly quickly because, as mammals, they need to breathe air and the nets drag them underwater, drowning them.

Recently, some of the largest tuna companies announced they would no longer buy any tuna that is caught in the same nets that trap dolphins. The companies have been using other methods to sight tuna, including detection equipment and watching birds that feed on dead fish that dolphins have eaten. Some of the fleets are also moving to waters where the tuna and dolphins do not mingle. There is also a law, the United States Marine Mammal Protection Act, that limits the number of dolphins that can be caught by the American tuna fleet. Some foreign fleets also go along with the law, but many more do not, and dolphins still die along with the tuna.

There are arguments on both sides of the issue here, too. Environmentalists believe, of course, that the dolphins, along with other marine mammals, should be protected and not killed. They feel that the limits on dolphin kills and the use of other methods to catch tuna are the best approach. Fishermen argue that the high cost of refitting their boats will drive them out of business, and that because the dolphins usually accompany schools of large tuna — the ones that are best for food — the ban on dolphin catching would force fishermen to go after smaller, immature fish. Think about this for a moment. Which is more important, protecting dolphins or providing consumers with an important source of fish? Is it worse to fish for small, immature tuna since the practice would stop them from reproducing and thereby reduce the supply? Wouldn't fishing just for small tuna upset the balance of nature? Should we force foreign countries to honor our limit law, especially countries that rely more on fish for food than we do? Again, we may be caught between a rock and a hard place on an environmental issue.

The plight of the dolphins does not end there, however. The playful mammals are also being killed off by pollution. Late in 1990, people who live near the sea in Italy, Spain, and France began noticing the bodies of dolphins floating offshore and washing up on the beaches. When doctors conducted autopsies on the dead mammals, they found high levels of PCBs and toxic metals. Not only that, but the dolphins had apparently been infected with a virus that causes a form of pneumonia; the virus, it appeared, was the same one that had killed thousands of seals in the North Sea some time before. The scientists suspected that the toxic chemicals somehow reduced the dolphins' tolerance for disease by weakening their immune systems. When that happened, it was easy for the virus to affect the dolphins.

Both freshwater and saltwater fish are also being threatened by various environmental hazards. While it can take many years to assess the extent and severity of environmental damage — as in the case of the Exxon *Valdez* spill — given what is known about the fragility of so many species and the toll pesticides like DDT have taken on wildlife, it is difficult to dismiss the adverse effects of pollution and other environmental attacks on fish.

While recreational and commercial fishing can deplete a stock of fish, it is mostly the destruction of their habitats that takes their lives. When fish are taken in large numbers it rarely causes extinction simply because fishermen generally quit when the fish stocks start thinning out. The remaining fish are thus given a chance to reproduce. But when overfishing is combined with some harmful practice — chemical dumping, generation of hydroelectric power, dam building, and so on — fish are definitely threatened because their homes are threatened.

In the northeastern United States and in Canada, the lakes and streams have become so tainted by acid rain that fish cannot live in them. The Georges Bank fishing grounds off New England, once among the world's richest fisheries, now have fewer cod and haddock. Wild stocks of the endangered aurora trout have been wiped out in 100,000 lakes in Ontario and Quebec, and half the range of the endangered Acadian whitefish of Nova Scotia has been destroyed. The eastern sand darter is threatened by silt pouring into streams, the eyeless northern cavefish by groundwater pollution from caves in Indiana and Kentucky; the spawning runs of the shortnosed sturgeon of the Atlantic Coast have been destroyed by damming of rivers.[4] Tumors have turned up in the livers of English sole that live on sediment, sediment that is often full of mercury, lead, zinc, cadmium, and PCBs. And fish of all kinds die when blooms of algae, caused as we have seen by the dumping of fertilizers into the water, steal oxygen from the water to create dead zones or release poisons fatal to fish. One especially vicious bloom in Japan's Inland Sea recently killed a million yellowtail tuna with a market value of some $15 million; in another dead zone off New Jersey, a million fluke and flounder died in oxygen-poor water. Yet another bloom killed millions of salmon and sea trout in Scandinavian breeding ponds; so widespread was the algae bloom that fish farmers had to tow the floating ponds from place to place in a desperate effort to outrun the algae.[5]

Crustaceans, the class of marine animals that includes crabs, lobsters, and shrimp, are also attacked by diseases that may be caused by pollutants. These hard-shelled creatures develop a disease that looks like leprosy. The affected crustaceans lose claws and develop jagged holes and black splotches in their shells. Though it is difficult to prove, many scientists believe that sewage sludge is the cause of this shell disease.

Pollutants injure fish, crustaceans, and marine mammals either by getting into their systems and killing them directly or by killing their food supplies. One interesting example of how disease may be transmitted in a marine mammal is recounted by Dr. Romona Haebler, a veterinary pathologist with the Environmental Protection Agency. It concerns a West Indian manatee, a walruslike mammal, which died in Florida of toxoplasmosis, a central nervous system disease caused by a parasite. The parasites begin their lives in cats and pass their eggs in the cats' feces. In this case, the theory is that infected cat litter was dumped into a household toilet, from which it entered the sewage system; it then drained into and contaminated the water where the manatee lived. Though manatees live in salt water, they like to drink fresh water and are often observed drinking from sewage plant discharge pipes. When the manatee drank the contaminated water, it contracted the disease.[6]

Sometimes, when female marine mammals eat contaminated food, the toxic compounds are stored in their body fat, especially in their milk. When the mammals nurse their young, they pass the contaminants on to their offspring. PCBs, a common class of contaminants found in marine animals, is among the chemicals that are stored in fat tissue.

Pollutants, land development, agricultural practices, and overzealous fishing are not the only human activities that endanger life on earth. Sometimes, other things that we do without thinking about the consequences are responsible. Consider, for a moment, the aquatic pest known as the zebra mussel. This mollusk — a member of a group that includes snails, clams, and octopuses — is so named because of the dark stripes on its shell. It is prevalent in much of Europe but had not been seen in large numbers in our country until very recently. The mussel, which reproduces swiftly and by the millions, has been turning up in the Great Lakes and in the Hudson and Mississippi rivers. It clogs the intake pipes of power, water treatment, and industrial plants, and it devours the microscopic plants at the bottom of the food chain.

How did the zebra mussel get here? Well, enter human beings. Scientists believe that zebra mussels were brought from infested ports overseas in the ballast water aboard oceangoing ships and dumped first in the Great Lakes in 1988. Because the zebra mussels have no natural enemies here, they are able to multiply rapidly.

Moving out of the water, we find that things are not much better onshore for wildlife. Whether they fly or walk, slither through the jungles or swing from trees, the creatures that live on or in the earth are hurting, some worse than others, because of our insensitivity. At least 1,000 mammals and birds are actually threatened or endangered — among them the tiger, giant panda, the blue whale, the California condor, the snow leopard, and the bald eagle, to name but a few of the better-known ones.

One way we endanger animals is overhunting. Hunting some wild animals for food, clothing, and even for sport is an ancient practice. When it is done for food and for skins, it is essential to the livelihood of many societies. Hunting for recreation is, or should be, carefully regulated so that only so many of a certain species are killed. Hunting laws are quite specific about what kinds of animals may be killed and about where and when.

But sometimes hunters overdo it. One glaring example is, of course, the elephant. Now confined to Asia and Africa, elephants are hunted for sport and for their ivory tusks. That ivory is useful and beautiful is obvious: it has been used to make all sorts of things, from piano keys to dice, from statues to earrings. Ivory is also expensive. Raw ivory costs about $150 a pound. In an attempt to safeguard the elephant, most governments have voted to outlaw the trading of ivory. That does not mean no one will be able to buy ivory anymore. Some countries — among them Hong Kong and some cash-poor African nations — do not go along with the ban and continue to deal in ivory. There is also a widespread illegal trade in ivory, and one doesn't have to look too hard to find it somewhere.

Elephant hunting raises questions just as whaling does. Should people in every country with an elephant population be allowed to kill the animals for their ivory? Or should the right to kill elephants be restricted to those countries with plenty of elephants? Is it better to place a limit on how many elephants can be killed and how much ivory any country can sell, rather than ban ivory outright? Since many African nations are so poor, what's wrong with allowing them to sell a unique, useful, and valuable resource in order to make money? Is protecting the elephant more important than giving the Africans a chance at a better way of life?

Again, we must point out that like fishing, hunting is not what is generally endangering our animals. Despite the clamor over fur coats, parrot feathers, and ivory, these are not the main causes of extinctions. In Africa and Asia, for instance, the elephants are running out of living space because farmers and city builders are taking over the land. It is the slashing and burning of the wildlife habitats that is mostly to blame for endangering our wildlife.

Here is how one noted ecology writer, Norman Myers, has addressed that point:

> Virtually all these extinctions are being caused through the indirect actions of humankind. We very rarely hunt a species to extinction. It is true that the dodo and the Steller sea cow, the passenger pigeon and the great auk, were driven over the edge through crass over-hunting as much as by any other factor. In our own age, we have seen a similar fate all but overtake the great whales (fortunately, the whales are now entering a more prosperous era, having been rescued virtually from the brink of extinction). But in the main, wild creatures are not eliminated through the poisoned arrows, the harpoons and the sporting rifles of modern man. Rather they are eliminated through the bulldozer, chainsaw and digging hoe. In Africa, comparatively little damage is being inflicted by the many thousands of spears and traps utilized by men who know they are breaking the law. Much more harmful are the millions of

digging hoes, wielded by people who are otherwise landless, and who believe they are doing no more than pursuing their legitimate needs as law-abiding citizens when they dig up the last habitats of zebras, giraffes and lions.[7]

The smallest land creatures, too, are made homeless or are killed by such activities. The slashing and burning that clears forests for logging and for agricultural land, as well as the dumping of pesticides and herbicides on fields — 2.6 million pounds of pesticides a year in the United States alone — are having an increasingly adverse effect on countless birds, plants, insects, and even soil bacteria. Too often we tend to overlook the tiniest creatures in favor of the more visible forms of life. These smaller wildlife forms may not be as imposing as a blue whale, a California condor, a redwood tree, or a mountain gorilla, but they are most certainly as vital to the ecosystem.

Consider birds. There are more than 9,000 known species, and over the years many of them, the frail and fluttery along with the eaglelike, have suffered immensely because of human activities. Destruction of tropical jungles and the indiscriminate use of DDT and other pesticides have killed them off. The casualty list is a long one. Here's a sampling: the Himalayan tragopan, endangered because the trees in which it lives are cut down for fuel; the California condor, endangered due to persecution by humans; the Eskimo curlew, endangered due to hunting; the Japanese crested ibis, due to defor-estation; the Spanish imperial eagle, due to persecution; Audouin's gull, due to egg hunting by humans; the earth-burrowing Bermuda cahow, due to pesticides; the Everglades kite, due to land reclamation in Florida's swampy grasslands, which has severely reduced its food supply of freshwater snails.[8] Ducks and geese, when they're not shot at or poisoned, face another obstacle to their survival: they often stay in an area year-round now because the watering places they ordi-narily visited on their way south in the winter have been filled in by land developers. While it might be nice to have these birds around, it's not normal for them, and as more and more of them stay, they soon run out of living space and food, and many die.

The peregrine falcon is perhaps one of the best examples of how a bird can be affected by some human activity. In the case of the peregrine, the spreading of pesticides is the activity. The peregrine is a very swift raptor — a bird of prey — that has also been used in the sport of falconry, the training of falcons to hunt game. Raptors are especially vulnerable to pesticide poisoning because they feed on food sources that are most apt to be contaminated, such as mice and other birds.

During the early 1960s, large numbers of peregrines and sparrow hawks began dying suddenly, and scientists eventually discovered that the cause was pesticide poisoning. The peregrines had fed on pigeons that had eaten seeds from fields coated with DDT and other insecticides. Scientists also found that the eggs laid by the peregrines had thin shells, which meant that when the female birds sat on the eggs to incubate and hatch them, the fragile eggs broke, preventing the birth of new falcons.

Because DDT contamination was so widespread, the peregrine falcons all but vanished from the northeastern United States and most of England. Populations of other raptors, including the bald eagle, also began to decline. After DDT was banned, some of the peregrines and eagles began to return, but their populations are not as large as they once were. Indeed, in Africa, where DDT is still used to destroy disease-causing mosquitoes and flies, peregrines, eagles, and other birds of prey are still being harmed. Should the Africans ban pesticides? It's easy enough to say yes because of what the pesticides do to birds and other wildlife. But when one considers that Africa has far more disease-bearing insects and other pests than we have, that answer may be a bit too simple. The Africans need to eradicate the pests if they are to protect themselves, their crops, and their farm animals from disease. Once again, we are damned if we do and damned if we don't.

About twenty species of insects, too, are endangered, although most of us would probably say good riddance. There are at least a million known insect species and undoubtedly many millions more, making them by far the largest group of animals on earth. There are perhaps 1,000 or more different kinds in your own backyard alone, a million and more to any given acre of land.

A few insects are pesty, even dangerous. Read any bottle of garden spray, and you'll have the names of only a few of the ones that can wreck our plants, flowers, and vegetables: cabbage maggots, Japanese beetles, leaf miners, red spider mites, and aphids. On a far more ominous note, some, such as mosquitoes and ticks, carry diseases, and at least twenty species are capable of creating an epidemic in humans. Biting gnats cause Oropouche fever, a serious tropical disease prevalent in the Amazon and Panama; wasp stings can cause severe allergic reactions; some spiders can kill humans with a bite. Many others, from boll weevils to locusts, devastate crops. Yes, there is no doubt that insects can make our lives miserable.

But the creepy crawlers are not all bad. In fact, many of them are so valuable that life would be a lot worse without them. By the process of pollination, insects give us fruits, nuts, vegetables, and cotton. We also get honey, dyes, wax, silk, and even shellac from insects. And insects provide food for birds, fish, and other animals. Scavenger insects feed on dead plants, animals, and dung, not only removing eyesores from the environment but enriching the soil by processing what they've eaten and returning it to the earth. Termites and carpenter ants, which can be holy terrors if they get into the wood of our homes, speed up the destruction of fallen trees and old logs and turn them into soil. Insects such as the praying mantis kill other insects, sometimes the ones that bother us the most. Other insects can destroy weeds and other growth that threaten our crops and overrun valuable land. Insects even have value in medicine and science. For instance, a beetle extract called cantharidin has been used to treat reproductive tract difficulties, and for hundreds of years, surgeons have known that the larvae of the blowfly can be used to eat away the dead tissue around wounds. In the laboratory, the fast-breeding fruit fly is widely used in genetics studies. Other insects, such as the ants, are marvelous models for studying behavior and social organization. And insects are barometers of the environment: when scientists want to know if a lake or river is polluted, they often check out the number of insects remaining.

Insects, then, are quite valuable to us, not only for what they do for us, but because they maintain the balance in nature that is so essential to all life. But kill some of them we must if we are to preserve our food supply and keep ourselves free from disease. So we have pesticides. The problem with these chemical weapons is that they usually work by poisoning an insect's nervous system, and that means they also poison the nervous systems of all other living creatures they come in contact with, including harmless insects. Pesticides are also responsible for the high rate of extinction among insects. Indeed, the insects suffer the greatest number of extinctions. One reason for this is that many tropical insects live only in specific forests or even in one kind of tree. Just one kind of tree may be home to thousands of different insects — not to mention birds, bacteria, and many other life-forms. Wiping out one forest or one kind of tree, then, can eradicate all those insects and other wildlife forever.

In light of what we know about the value of insects, dealing with them is complicated. If we continue to wipe out insects that we know have value, we're destroying a benefit. We're also destroying the many millions of species we don't know about, and perhaps these have even more value. The only way we're going to find out about these unknown species is to let them live until we can identify them. Indiscriminate use of pesticides, therefore, is like burning a reference book before we read it. Whenever we eradicate a species of insect — or of any other living thing — we are losing a very special natural resource, one that has taken thousands of millions of years to get to where it is and that plays a key ecological role. The genes that are present in all those species are arranged in unique codes that can be translated into something useful by the phenomenal process known as genetic engineering. Special genes can be removed from a life-form, copied in the laboratory, and grown in quantity to make a drug or some other useful product.

But can we afford to let the insects alone, given what we know about the damage many of them cause to us, to animals, and to our plants and crops? Some insects may even be destroying rare and valuable plants, just as humans are doing. Should we get rid of the insects if that means saving some plants? Or should we forget the plants and save the insects? Which is more valuable?

The only answer to that last question is neither. Both are equally valuable. Plants and forests, too, are important resources and vital members of the ecological community. When we destroy them with herbicides or alter their growing patterns by changing the climate with air pollution, we are upsetting nature's balance just as when we destroy insects or any other animals. Speaking of the makeup of the forest, the noted American botanist Clarence J. Hylander has written:

> From the ecological point of view, the forest cannot be described as an arithmetical equation of 25 trees + 20 birds + 10 mammals = 55 kinds of wildlife = the forest. Instead, the forest is considered a living unit within which definite functions are assigned to certain types of plants and animals. Such a unit of nature, consisting of organisms living together in the same environment, is known as a biotic community. This community has a definite membership, it is characterized by definite physical living conditions, and consists of an internal organization with mutually dependent organisms forming a complex "web of life."[9]

As sources of food for man and beast, of fuel, building materials, pulp for paper, shade for the ferns and mosses that require it to live, and oxygen to enable us to live, as homes for birds and other animals, wild plants are high on the list of the most valuable raw materials we know. The names of our fruits and vegetables are household words. But there are thousands of other edible plants and fruits, some of them more nutritious than our relatively small variety of usual fare, and every day, it seems, we hear of some new food source — new to us, perhaps — growing in the wild, or we learn that scientists are making a better one. There is the Brazilian pupunha palm, chock full of vitamins, protein, minerals, oil, and carbohydrates, a complete food if there ever was one. A grain obtained from a Mexican marine plant can be ground into flour. People eat the desert prickly pear, the beach plum, seaweed, hearts of palm, lotus roots, daisy leaves, even ice cream made from soybeans. Chances are that if it grows it is food for someone, animal or human. And if it isn't growing right now, just wait awhile. Scientists can make things happen with plants that Mother Nature has been unable to. For instance, by transplanting genes from a form of corn that resists drought and disease to a tastier variety that doesn't, they can create a new, delicious form of corn that is stronger than before.

We also get many valuable drugs from plants that grow on the land and in the sea. In fact, aspirin was first extracted from the bark of willow trees. The painkiller morphine comes from opium poppies; curare, an arrowhead poison extracted from a vine and used by South American Indians, is also used in medicine as a muscle relaxant; the Indian snakeroot plant gives us tranquilizers and the nightshade plant gives us atropine, a powerful antispasmodic; vincristine, used to treat cancer, is derived from the Madagascar periwinkle. If you add in all the herbs and roots from angelica to yarrow that cure or are supposed to cure all our ailments, tooth decay to flu, there is quite a well-stocked pharmacy growing in the wild.

Even the lowliest lichens — a combination of fungus and alga — are important to us all. Among the earliest of the earth's inhabitants, lichens are just about everywhere — in the desert, in ponds and oceans, in tropical jungles, on mountaintops, even in frigid Antarctica. They are among the few organisms that can convert nitrogen gas to the form used as food by trees and other plants. Lichens with blue-green algae, for example, convert more than half of the nitrogen consumed by the Douglas fir forests of the northwestern United States. In addition to their ecological role, lichens are valuable in other ways. Lichens are used to color Harris tweeds, and they also produce about 500 compounds unknown in any other plant group, among them anticancer compounds and several acids. Finally, scientists can measure the decline of lichens in an area to determine the degree of air pollution.[10]

But for all the benefits Earth derives from plants, many of them are endangered, just as the animals are. For some reason, perhaps because they don't seem really "alive" to many people, plants seem to get short shrift when they're competing for attention with the likes of pandas and porpoises. Many of us truly do not see the whole forest for the trees. Keep the entire ecosystem in mind when you're tempted to think that way. In fact, plants, insects, and soil bacteria may be even more vital to life on earth than some of the familiar endangered animals.

Farming, deforestation, land development, PCBs, and DDT all have a hand in the slow destruction of plants. And often when we cut plants out of an area, we make room for new opportunists — all manner of weeds and grasses that had once been kept in check where they ordinarily lived but now are free to run wild because their natural enemies are not around in the new habitat. These renegade plants eventually take over an area, wiping out the native species and changing the ecosystem.

To paraphrase what an old bit of verse says about weeds, our plants have been hunted and hacked and hoed to death and never draw a peaceful breath. By the end of 1990, the largest remaining parcel of virgin prairie in northeastern Kansas was plowed under. At one time, nearly 200 million acres of tall-grass prairie filled with hundreds of species of plants covered North America; today, only about 2 percent remains.[11] In Madagascar, more than 90 percent of the original vegetation has disappeared; in Central and South America, 15 percent of the plants have been characterized as among the living dead.[12]

People used to wonder why plants seemed to have escaped the mass extinctions that wiped out the dinosaurs and other animals. One answer was that plants have the ability to regenerate quickly from stumps, roots, seeds, and spores. Things are different nowadays. Harvard biologist Andrew Knoll sees it this way:

> Today, after four hundred million years of increasing diversity in vascular plants (green plants such as ferns and seed plants), we seem to be on the brink of losing twenty percent or more of that diversity within a hundred years. What's important is not that all species will go extinct. We know they will; statistically, almost every species that has ever existed is now extinct. What's important is that the loss of twenty percent of diversity in a hundred years is a remarkable event on a geological time scale.[13]

SOME SOLUTIONS

As biologist Paul R. Ehrlich of Stanford University has written:

Nothing is more important to human beings today than understanding how nature works. The very future of our society depends on whether Homo sapiens can learn to live without damaging the machinery of nature so seriously that it can no longer support civilization. Therefore, no science, indeed no aspect of human culture, is more important than ecology — the study of the interactions among organisms and between organisms and their physical environments.[14]

Ehrlich goes on to say that when we are familiar with basic ecology we will never again see plants, microorganisms, and animals, including people, as isolated things. Instead, we will see them as parts of a huge complex of natural machinery.

If we want to save our wildlife and all of the ecosystems that drive this earth, we must begin by appreciating that machinery of nature. Without knowing something about all of the interactions that take place in nature, we will have a difficult time understanding what sudden change can do to a fragile ecosystem.

For many years, the changes that humans brought about were not too devastating, outside of a few remote environments. But now, fortunately, there is a growing realization that if what humans are doing to the earth, water, and air is not checked, the balancing act that goes on throughout nature will be severely disrupted and the problems will be worldwide. Some people have argued that if we wait long enough diversity in nature will recover, even to such a degree that there could be more diversity than before. The problem with that reasoning, according to Dr. Knoll, is that the time scale for such a recovery is around ten million years. "So the diversity that we lose over the next hundred years," he explains, "is not only lost to our grandchildren, but it's also lost for the foreseeable duration of the species."[15] So, what steps can we take now to protect our wildlife?

First, pesticide use and abuse should be reduced. This is the responsibility of pesticide makers, as well as of the farmers and even the home gardeners who use the potent chemicals.

The key to pesticide use is selectivity, that is, using a pesticide that will kill only the harmful insects and not the ones that are important in so many ways. In other words, instead of dropping a bombload of some pesticide on an area and taking out the good insects with the bad ones, a "bullet" approach that goes right to the target is far safer for the environment and more apt to spare our endangered wildlife.

This is why there is intense interest these days in so-called natural pesticides. These work by interfering with the way certain insects reproduce, mature, and hunt out and even taste food. For example, some years ago, at the University of California at Berkeley, Dr. Isao Kubo, a natural products chemist, isolated and identified biologically active chemicals from African medicinal plants. He and his associates found two compounds that cause pink bollworm and fall armyworm caterpillars — common pests in American cotton fields — to starve to death. The chemicals interfered with the caterpillars' molting, or skin-shedding, process. "When we force-fed the compounds to the caterpillars," Dr. Kubo explained,

> they failed to shed part of their skin. As a result, excess skin, looking like a helmet, stuck to the caterpillars' heads. The extra "head" prevented the caterpillars from moving and eating. After two to three days, they starved to death.[16]

It was not the first time Dr. Kubo came up with a natural pesticide. Another one from an African jungle plant prevents insects from devouring plants. It works by blocking the nerve signals that go from the insect's taste buds to its brain. As a result, the insect cannot experience taste and loses its desire to eat. Eventually, it starves to death.[17]

Another approach to insect control is with an ingredient called an IGR, an insect growth regulator. This one works on insects such as flea larvae that crawl about unseen in carpets and blankets where dogs and cats sleep. The substance imitates a so-called juvenile hormone that the larvae make themselves as they develop into adult fleas. An IGR changes the timing of the larvae's development so that they never grow into biting fleas.[18]

Along with developing pesticides that work in natural ways, several companies manufacture alternative substances that can kill but are not toxic to the environment. One approach is the use of a "living insecticide," bacteria or viruses that kill destructive insects but leave others alone. Another common remedy is diatomaceous earth, which is derived from the shells of microscopic, one-celled plants that were around millions of years ago in the primitive oceans. When they died, they left behind particles of the shells that protected them. The shells contain crystals of silica, a mineral used to make glass and ceramics. So sharp are the minute shell bits that they pierce the insects' bodies, draining them of the fluid they need to survive. Diatomaceous earth is not a hazard to other living things.

Biodegradable pesticides are also in use. These kill insects without injuring birds, animals, or plants. Another alternative pesticide uses pheromones, harmless chemicals that are produced by the insects themselves. Some insects use pheromones to stimulate other insects or to leave trails that lead to food or home. As more and more insects become resistant to pesticides such as DDT, scientists are baiting pesticides with pheromones to lure specific insects to the poison. Even the zebra mussel we talked about may someday be controlled with a harmless version of a common chemical element, potassium. Called potassium phosphate, the mussel killer is lethal to the marine pests but apparently harmless to most other freshwater animals. Other possible ways to control the zebra mussel are under study, including the use of sound waves to scare them off and substances that stop them from attaching themselves or their larvae to the pipes they favor.

Better protection of wildlife habitats is also essential. This obviously includes monitoring what we dump into our rivers, streams, lakes, and oceans, and our farmlands and forests. Habitat protection also means paying more attention to how many dams we build, how many wetlands we drain, and how many forests we cut down — then weighing such practices against the need. Development should also be what ecologists refer to as sustainable — that is, resources should not be used up faster than nature can replenish them.

Habitat protection needs better regulation, too. The Endangered Species Act of 1973 forbids the federal government from funding any human activities that could damage a plant or animal on the endangered species list. But some environmentalists say the law is not strictly enforced. Also, it takes time for a species to get on the endangered list, sometimes so long that a species might become extinct before it is declared eligible for protection.

Perhaps we ought to expand the national park system as a way of protecting wildlife habitats, or we ought to save as many species as possible in zoos and aquariums. Perhaps we can find new ways to get endangered areas to yield something we need without destroying them. One example of that last possibility: making paper from kenaf, an African plant that can produce five times as much pulp per acre than the trees that are ordinarily cut for newsprint.[19]

Habitat protection is not just for faraway rain forests or deep-sea coral reefs, either. Property owners and gardeners can help, too. They can plant buffer strips of natural plants along stream banks and lakeshores, they can ask contractors to leave as many trees as possible when preparing a building site, and they can apply fertilizers and pesticides with care.[20]

More education and research are important, too. More people have to learn about wildlife conservation, about the needs of different species and about their roles in the ecosystem. Even a tiny space in someone's backyard deserves such attention. As the noted physician and "biology watcher" Dr. Lewis Thomas has expressed it:

> Viewed from the distance of the moon, the astonishing thing about the earth, catching the breath, is that it is alive. The photographs show the dry, pounded surface of the moon in the foreground, dead as an old bone. Aloft, floating free beneath the moist, gleaming membrane of bright blue sky, is the rising earth, the only exuberant thing in this part of the cosmos. . . . It has the organized, self-contained look of a live creature, full of information, marvelously skilled in handling the sun.[21]

Is that not enough to make us want to protect our wildlife?

10
THE PROBLEM:

POVERTY AND OVERPOPULATION

Ultimately, as we have seen, human activities are to blame for the state of the environment. Human beings pollute, dump garbage, fell trees, disrupt the ozone layer, and destroy ecosystems and the millions of plant and animal species that dwell within them.

Humans affect the environment in yet another way, one that may not seem as dramatic as the releasing of CFCs into the atmosphere or the radiation accidents at Chernobyl and Three Mile Island, but one which is just as devastating, if not more so. The twin threats of poverty and rapid population growth, too often intertwined, also put the entire planet at grave risk. Indeed, the combination may well be the most serious of the many problems that menace the environment.

Some numbers will help you understand why. In 1900, the world's population stood at around 1.5 billion. Today, it is now estimated to be around 5.3 billion, with China far and away the leader with nearly 1.2 billion people and a growth rate of some 15 million more every year. At present, the world's population is increasing by three people every second — about a quarter million each day. According to the United Nations Population Fund, some 96 million people — an extra Thailand and Korea — will be added every year, with a whole extra China over the decade. During the next century, world population is expected to more than double, a serious and significant enough increase alone but one that becomes more ominous considering that 90 percent of that increase will take place in the poorer, developing countries of the world, the countries that are the least able to handle it. The African countries, especially, will feel the crush: over the next quarter-century, Nigeria's population will rise from 112 million to 274 million and that of Kenya from 23 million to 79 million.[1]

As population expands in the developing nations, so, too, will the number of their poor and hungry. Already, poverty is on a sharp rise in Africa, Latin America, and parts of Asia. According to the World-watch Institute, more than 200 million people have joined the ranks of the poor since 1980; as of today, approximately 1.2 billion people, nearly a fourth of humankind, do not have their basic needs met.[2] This fact is noteworthy since global per capita income — the average amount of money earned by one person — has more than doubled since midcentury among the more fortunate.

Here's how Alan Durning, a senior researcher at Worldwatch, has described the difference between the haves and the have-nots:

> The world has 157 billionaires and perhaps 2 million million-aires, but 100 million people around the globe are homeless, living on sidewalks, in garbage dumps, and under bridges. Americans spend five billion dollars each year on special diets to lower their calorie consumption, while the world's poorest 400 million people are so undernourished they are likely to suffer stunted growth, mental retardation, or death. As water from a single spring in France is bottled and shipped to the prosperous around the world, 1.9 billion people drink and bathe in water contaminated with deadly parasites and disease-causing bacteria and viruses, and more than half of humanity lacks sanitary toilets.[3]

Most of the world's poor are rural villagers in the underdeveloped world, and most of these — two-thirds by some counts — are children under the age of fifteen. The poor quite often have very large families. One apparent reason for this is that poor couples sometimes see children as a way to increase the family's means of support. This sort of strength-in-numbers approach may keep the family poor, but it also might help them avoid starvation since there are more family members doing different things to help feed the group. The strategy does not always work, however. Plagued by disease and deprived of adequate nourishment and clean water, about a third of the children die before their fifth birthday; the ones who survive are often physically stunted — that is, their growth is halted — and mentally damaged because they so often went hungry during the crucial growth years of six months to two years.

How does all of this affect the environment? After all, a country's people should be a valuable resource, not a problem. In general, the more people there are, the greater the drain on every resource — land, forests, water supplies, and energy. This is especially true in the rural Third World, where the people rely heavily on the soil for food, on streams for drinking, washing clothes, and bathing, and on forests for fuel and building materials. As the population increases, these resources are overused until they are either depleted or, as in the case of water, so spoiled as to be unfit for human consumption. Sometimes, because hard-pressed farmers try to increase their livestock herds, the animals rapidly thin out the precious grasslands. When that occurs, not only does the vegetation necessary for grazing dwindle, but so, too, does the amount of enriching organic matter that the animals are supposed to put back into the soil.

Farmers also sometimes drill too many wells in order to provide water for their livestock. Such overpumping often removes more water from the ground than can flow back in. Two-thirds of South Africans use wood for fuel, a practice that eats up about 1,800 pounds of wood a year per person. It is easy to see how such a high rate of burning would strip forests quickly. Indeed, some forests in the region lost all their trees in just twenty years. Forests in the developing countries are also chopped down for another reason: to make room for cropland for the increasing population. It has been said that population growth is responsible for a far greater share of deforestation than logging by timber companies and that expanding populations may, in fact, be responsible for more than 85 percent of the loss of forest cover.

One should not be too harsh on the people who live in these areas.

They may be ruining the environment, but not because they are malicious or ignorant. They do so because they have often been pushed to the very edge of poverty, and even starvation, and have no other way out. A farmer may be too poor to buy fertilizers or the equipment that many well-off farmers use to conserve their land, and so when he overworks his land he eventually ruins it. In South Africa, apartheid — the racist policy that has separated whites from blacks and forces blacks to live in poverty — has helped to devastate the country's landscape. Forced to live in overcrowded reserves called homelands — pieces of land where topsoil is thin, the ground rocky and sloping, and rainfall scarce — it is no wonder that the people in such an already forbidding environment wear down the land even more, literally to the bare rock, in order to survive.

Such last-ditch activities are not going on just in Africa. Consider the case of Abu and Sharifa, heads of a family in Bangladesh, an Asian country near India. After suffering a number of misfortunes — famine, illness, and the loss of land in a family dispute — they had to sell off what land they had left, as well as a cow, furniture, jewelry, and farm equipment. In the end, they had to cut down the only two trees they owned to sell them for firewood and earn the money they needed so desperately. "There is no rice in my household," said Abu, "and I have six children to feed. In June I cut my mango tree, and now I am chopping up my jackfruit tree. My children will never eat fruit — how can I afford to buy it in the bazaar? Rich people in this country don't understand how my stomach burns."[4] Sadly, as resources disappear or are damaged, poverty increases because there is soon nothing left to feed and warm the population.

More people also means the creation of more heat from all the burning of wood and fossil fuels, heat that will spur the greenhouse effect and may produce dramatic climate changes. It has been estimated that population growth alone accounted for nearly two-thirds of the increase in carbon dioxide gas — the most important of the greenhouse gases — that entered the atmosphere between 1950 and 1955. As the population increases, as it is expected to do, the output of carbon dioxide from the Third World alone will be enormous: people in those parts of the globe will be producing an average of 1.7

tons of the gas per person every year by the year 2025, more than double the current level.[5]

More people means more waste, too, both chemical and human, as well as more pollution. From the swollen sewage drains of crowded Calcutta to the bursting slums and shantytowns of Africa, stinking heaps of garbage and other refuse, including toxic waste, already exist alongside people, far too close for comfort and health. It is estimated that when the world's population reaches the ten-billion mark, we will generate about 400 million tons of solid waste a year, enough to bury major cities such as Los Angeles under hundreds of feet of trash.

The overcrowded and the poor not only contribute to the decay of the environment, but they are hugely affected by what they do to their surroundings, too. The livelihoods of hundreds of millions of people not as well off as those in the industrialized nations are already at risk because of desertification, deforestation, and soil erosion; shortages of fuel wood affect another 100 million or more.

The rich are, of course, subjected to the same environmental hazards as the poor, for the entire earth and all its people are, after all, under siege. Pollution is pollution to human beings whether they live near a toxic waste dump or in a tree-lined suburb. But it is nonetheless true that the poor and those who live in overcrowded conditions suffer far more exposure to pollution and hazardous materials than do those who are better off, if only because they cannot afford to live very far from the sources of environmental disaster. Virtually all of the victims of the Bhopal accident were poor, people who could not live anywhere but near the smokestacks. It has been demonstrated that the poorer a neighborhood, and the darker the skin of its residents, the more apt the neighborhood is to be near a waste dump. Nor does one have to go only to Africa or India to see this phenomenon. "Three-fourths of hazardous waste landfills in the American Southeast are in low-income, black neighborhoods," says Alan Durning of Worldwatch,

and more than half of all black and Hispanic Americans live in communities with at least one toxic waste site. In the United

States as in the Third World, the rich get richer and the poor get poisoned.[6]

Even away from the belching factories and the noxious waste dumps, the poor are at risk. Their crowded shacks are filled with choking smoke from old-fashioned cookstoves, fumes that put them at high risk of respiratory diseases and cancer.

To say that the environment in which the poor live has an effect on their health and welfare is not strong enough. The poorest countries in the world have higher rates of infectious and parasitic diseases and of malnutrition. The dirty water they are forced to drink — and dirty water is the world's major cause of disease — leads to a billion cases of diarrhea a year and more than 200 million cases of schistosomiasis, a serious disease caused by parasitic worms carried by snails that live in the water.

There are other problems that come with a degraded environment. If the ozone layer continues to be depleted, for example, everyone will be affected. But the poor who live and work on open farmlands will feel the full force of the sun's ultraviolet rays on their health and well-being. As heat rises and rainfall decreases because of the greenhouse effect, the earth's most fertile agricultural areas will dry up, crops will fail, and the poor, who have a hard enough time surviving, will be in worse shape because they will have fewer and fewer cash crops to sell.

Finally, there are the many social problems that a degraded environment brings. The inadequate housing that is so prevalent in the ravaged areas of the world leads to more social strains, and assaults such as child abuse, rape, and incest increase. Also, as more and more people are pushed off their land, they head for the cities in search of more opportunity and better housing. The migration may take some of the pressure off the wasted environment and give the overworked land some time to recover, but it makes things worse for the cities. Too often, the people who flee the farms for a better life end up living on the streets or in grubby squatter settlements, even worse off than before.

SOME SOLUTIONS

How can we remedy overpopulation and poverty and thus help save the environment?

The easy answer, of course, is to reduce the world's population and totally wipe out poverty. If there were fewer people on this earth, and if everyone had the same rights and opportunities, chances·are our precious natural resources would benefit enormously, not to mention the people of every nation.

But how do we do it? Like many of the solutions that have been offered throughout this book, that is far easier said than done.

Young people I have talked with offered a few solutions:

"It won't always be a problem because there are wars, and they kill lots of people. Maybe the wars we will always have will take care of everything."

"There should be more birth control. People should be ordered to have no more than two children."

"We should legalize abortion. Too many children are being born for countries to take care of."

"We should do operations to stop certain people from having children."

"Men should learn that women are for more than just having children. If women had equal rights to men they wouldn't all be having kids because they'd be out working more and wouldn't just see themselves as baby machines."

Before you agree too quickly with one or more of these suggestions, you'd best have a little more information. Let's look at the suggestion about war. First of all, war is not glorious, no matter how stirring the battle hymns nor how exciting all those heroic war movies. War is violent and bloody, a solution, if it may be called that, that leaves many scars, on people and on countries. As Benjamin Franklin put it, "There never was a good war or a bad peace." Civil War general William Tecumseh Sherman said it another way:

War is at best barbarism. . . . Its glory is all moonshine. It is only those who have neither fired a shot nor heard the shrieks and groans of the wounded who cry aloud for blood, more vengeance, more desolation. War is hell.

It is true that many people are killed in wars. The Soviet Union, for example, lost at least 20 million people during World War II, an appallingly high number. But right after the war, childbearing rose, then rose even more when the Soviet government adopted a number of measures to stimulate it.[7] It is also true that many people die from natural causes, from accidents, and from diseases — far more than are usually killed in wars — and the problem of overpopulation is still with us. Thirty million people died of influenza throughout the world in the great epidemic of 1918 to 1919, an enormous number, but it did nothing to slow the steady growth of the population. Two million children die every year of measles alone, and that has not had any effect either. Even if you added in deaths from wars, not enough people would die — not unless one were to wipe out most of the world with nuclear bombs — to make up for the increasing number of births. The fact is, the sheer size of the population in many countries only guarantees that there will be enormous increases in the population as the existing population also has children. In China, for example, half the population is now twenty-five years of age or younger, which means that that large segment of the population is either producing children now or will soon do so.

Birth control, or family planning as the practice is referred to, seems to be the only obvious and acceptable answer to halting the population explosion. In fact, according to the United Nations Population Fund, if the use of family planning does not increase, the world could be headed for a total of 14 billion people in the next century.

There are three methods of family planning, but not all of them are acceptable, or accessible, to everyone. They are contraception, abortion, and sterilization. Another method once widespread among many primitive tribes, and in China and India, was infanticide. This is the killing of newborn children by a parent or someone with the parent's consent. In ancient Greece and Rome, deformed infants were put to death to rid the population of "undesirables," and in China and India, for economic and religious reasons, female children were most often killed. Today, fortunately, the laws of all nations treat infanticide as a crime. That does not mean that infanticide is never practiced. From time to time, we hear reports that it is still going on in China and other countries.

Birth control pills taken by women, condoms worn by men during sexual intercourse, and devices called IUDs (intrauterine devices), which are inserted into a woman's uterus to prevent a fertilized egg from developing into an embryo are among the popular methods of contraception. Some women wear diaphragms, rubber caps that are fitted over the cervix to prevent sperm from entering the uterus. Men and women may also have operations that make them sterile, that is, unable to father or bear children. Sterilization is the most common means of birth control in the world; 119 million women have had the operation, 45 million men. IUDs are the second most popular method of birth control, with 84 million female users, and the birth control pill is third, with 67 million users. So-called natural methods of birth control, like the rhythm method, work by limiting sexual relations to those times when a woman is unlikely to conceive. Rhythm is the only method, outside of not having sex at all, that the Catholic Church allows.

While such methods of family planning are well known — and though birth control is generally recognized as a necessity as well as a legal and social right — the use of contraceptives varies greatly between countries, and even within countries. For many years, in fact, the whole idea of birth control was strongly opposed by poor countries whose leaders saw it as a trick by the more prosperous nations, a way to keep down the numbers of certain races. That notion has changed, and almost all of the Third World countries now recognize the need to check population growth. According to the United Nations, at least half the couples in those countries practice some form of modern contraception, compared with far fewer twenty-five years ago. As a result, many countries have succeeded in lowering their birth rates.

But problems still exist because the quality of contraceptive services and counseling varies so widely from country to country and not everyone has easy access to information or the contraceptives themselves. For example, while contraceptives and advice about how to use them are readily available to everyone in Europe and North America, not everyone agrees on whether unmarried minors should have access to birth control services without the knowledge or consent of their parents. The best family planning services and information in the developing world are available in East Asia, but this is not so in Latin America, where the only accepted method has long been periodic abstinence from sex.[8] Religious objections are generally behind such opposition to family planning in Central and South America, where Roman Catholics are a strong presence, and in parts of the Middle East, where stern Islamic moral views also hold that having children should be the goal of sex. There are other difficulties. Men in developing countries often have a macho image of themselves, and many of them often refuse to use condoms because they feel they weaken their masculine images. One recent survey in Kenya found that more men know about family planning than women and that a third of the men have never discussed it with their wives. Moreover, the Kenyan women feared their husbands would beat them if they were discovered to be using birth control.

Women in these poorer countries also find it difficult to use diaphragms because clean water for washing the devices is so hard to come by. Voluntary sterilization, the most widespread fertility control method in the world, is hardly ever performed in Africa, perhaps because surgical services are not always up to high standards, perhaps because of cultural reasons.

Even where contraceptives are fully acceptable, there are obstacles to population control. One of the biggest is the lack of money. Many Third World countries are so poor and in such debt that they simply cannot afford to spend much on family planning services. Moreover, money provided for such services from outside sources has dwindled. A reason for that is the controversy over whether to support a more controversial form of family planning, abortion. The U.S. contribution to international population-assistance programs declined 20 percent between 1985 and 1987, to around $230 million — and it has been suggested that former President Reagan's antiabortion policies were behind the decrease in America's generosity.

There is no question that abortion, which is the expulsion of a fetus from a mother's womb before it has fully developed, is the most hotly debated of all the methods of birth control. On one side are those who oppose the practice on religious and moral grounds; among these are the Catholic Church, fundamentalist Protestants and Muslims, and some Orthodox Jews. You have probably read a lot lately about people who are strongly against abortion because they believe that a fetus, even in its earliest stages, is a human being and that aborting it is murder. Those who feel this way are members of so-called pro-life movements, an unfortunate name choice because it implies that those who believe in abortion are against life. On the other side are those who feel that abortion is not a crime, that the developing fetus is not a human being, that abortion should be available at the request of a woman — the pro-choice argument — and that it is essential if the population is to be kept at safe limits.

There are valid arguments on both sides, and it is not our purpose here to favor one over the other. You should know, however, that abortion is legal and available to the majority of the world's population. There are different restrictions, though. About 24 percent of the world's people live in countries where abortion is allowed only to save the pregnant woman's life or is banned altogether. In this category are most of the Muslim countries of Asia, two-thirds of Latin America, half the countries of Africa, and three countries in Europe — Belgium, Ireland, and Malta.

Another 13 percent live in places that allow abortion for medical reasons — including protection of the woman's health, and sometimes when the fetus is damaged or at risk of being damaged. Twenty-four percent of the people are in countries that consider social factors — low income, poor housing, and being unmarried — in the decision to allow abortion. Among these countries are India, Japan, most of the countries in Eastern Europe, Germany, and the United Kingdom. Finally, 39 percent live in countries where the laws allow abortion on request. In these countries — the United States, China, France, Italy, the Soviet Union, and the Scandinavian countries — abortion is usually limited to the first three months of pregnancy. However, sometimes in these countries abortions for medical reasons may be allowed beyond the three-month limit.[9]

One problem with abortion is that the procedure is not always done under ideal medical conditions. When it is performed by trained personnel it is relatively safe and may even be much safer than childbirth. But where abortion is illegal, too often untrained people are called upon to perform the procedure. Indeed, a third of the pregnant women who die in the world do so because of the complications of an illegal abortion.

One of the suggestions that was made earlier when we asked how overpopulation and poverty could be eliminated had to do with improving the status of women. If that could be done, goes the argument, women would be more apt to seek family planning advice.

The fact that women are not as well off as men in the underdeveloped countries may be surprising to many people. Here's what Alan Durning has said about that inequality:

> The poor are more likely to be female than male, particularly in urban areas, leading some analysts to speak of a global "feminization of poverty." Although the true extent of female poverty remains uncertain, there is no question that life is harsher for poor women than for poor men.
>
> Women's burdens multiply endlessly. They are paid less than men — in Egypt, half as much for farm labor. But they work more — one to three additional hours each day, according to studies of villages in four countries. They are less educated — female literacy trails male literacy by 38 percentage points on average in the world's worst-off countries — but bear greater responsibility for the health of children.
>
> Women are expected to give birth to, raise, and feed numerous (preferably male) offspring, and consequently grow weak and ailing as their bodies are exhausted by the cycle of repeated pregnancy and childbirth. They are often abused and beaten at home, but have few legal rights and fewer property rights. They cannot leave their husbands unless they are willing to lose their social standing, economic security, and their children. For poor women, as a peasant woman from the Brazilian state of Minas Gerais says, "The only holiday is when you are asleep."[10]

African women, among others, would agree wholeheartedly with that last statement. In Africa, women are responsible for 70 percent of food production, as well as for child rearing and housework. This work load leads African women to take their daughters out of school to help with the chores. Girls out of school are more likely to marry at a young age, and they have more children.

If the key to population control and to lessening poverty in the developing countries lies in making conditions better for women and in giving them better access to birth control, women will need more opportunity for education. According to the United Nations' population experts, in 1986, 56 percent of the secondary-school-age girls in Latin America received an education; the figures were 39 percent in the Arab states, 33 percent in Asia, and 21 percent in Africa. Indeed, women make up almost two-thirds of the illiterate adults in developing countries; in 1985, only 51 percent of women could read, compared to 72 percent of men.

There are many benefits, of course, to an education. In Africa, for instance, women with seven years of education tend to marry four years later and have 2.2 fewer children than women with no formal education. Moreover, educated women in Africa are four times more likely to use contraception than their uneducated sisters.

Some years ago, the government of Bangladesh began giving organizations of village women loans to help them start small businesses; the women made pottery to sell, raised chickens, and operated grocery stores. Every week, the women received information about contraceptives. Today, 75 percent of the women in the cooperative use contraceptives — compared to only 35 percent of the women throughout the country.[11]

It is obvious that birth control is a key element in stopping population growth. But you may want to consider how abortion and contraceptives should be used in family planning. Should abortion be allowed in overpopulated poor countries with inadequate health care facilities, despite the fact that many young women will die at the hands of unskilled practitioners? What restrictions would you put on abortions? Is distributing contraceptives to everyone who wants them the same as providing abortion on request? If not, what do you feel is the difference? Consider the Soviet Union, where there are 70 million women of childbearing age. The country has no factories producing modern contraceptives, but abortion is available on demand, and many women must choose abortion among their limited options. Would it be better to provide more contraceptives to stop widespread abortion? On the other hand, should all countries have the same kind of family planning programs? Are you in favor of forcing families to limit the number of children they should have? China, for example, began a one-family, one-child program some years ago. People are given money every month and better housing if they follow the rule and are punished by fines or loss of jobs if they do not. Does such a policy promote abortion among women who may become pregnant for a second or third time? Would infanticide become commonplace again as families decide it is better to avoid punishment and be paid the extra money even though it means getting rid of extra children? And what about sterilization? The operation that makes a man or woman sterile is usually voluntary. Should poor people be forced to have the operation so that they cannot produce more children? This has happened in the past in some countries. Ask, too, if family planning alone is really enough to wipe out poverty and bring about economic improvement. It cuts down population growth, but does that necessarily mean poverty will also disappear? Or do we need something more? Can local efforts make a big difference in slowing population growth and alleviating poverty, or should something be done on a much larger scale, by national governments, for example?

Such questions must be asked, because eliminating overpopulation and poverty is crucial if we are to stop the spoiling of our environment. But it should be obvious, once again, that solving the problem is not easy. No environmental threat is going to be wiped away overnight, or by one method. In the last analysis, it all comes down to first raising public awareness of the dangers and then getting the public to change its habits. The first part of that proposition is fairly easy. The second is not. As we have said, many poor farming cultures regard children as vital to the survival of the family. Some men in those cultures also feel that having a lot of children is a sign of masculinity and power. Changing such deeply held views is a monumental task, but it can be done if people can be made to understand that the quality of life for people in any given society is far more important than their quantity. To get people to see that requires a concerted effort to give the poor more opportunities to learn and earn, opportunities equal to those offered to those who are more fortunate. It all requires a strategy, a commitment on a national and an international level. As we have tried to point out in this book, while the devastation of the environment may sometimes seem to be localized — an oil spill here, a nuclear accident there, a rain forest chopped down far away — it really does affect us all in some way. If poverty and overpopulation contribute to the degradation of the environment, the damage will not necessarily be confined to faraway places such as Africa; it will inevitably affect us all as the climate changes and space for living comfortably over the entire earth shrinks. If that is the case, then the solutions are everyone's responsibility.

Too often, as we have seen, people believe that the only solutions will come from the "hard" sciences such as chemistry, physics, biology, and engineering, to name a few. Science and technology have, of course, given us solutions to some of our environmental problems and will continue to do so. In the case of overpopulation, for example, research into new and more safe and effective methods of contraception must continue. Even now, scientists have come up with a new drug for women that induces abortion quickly — and more safely than through surgery. Capsules containing birth control drugs may now be inserted into a woman's arm, protecting her from an unwanted pregnancy for up to five years.

But there is another kind of science that is too often ignored when it comes to problems like those that threaten the environment. Known as social science, it is the branch of science that includes political science, economics, and sociology and that deals with how society and its institutions function and with how people relate to one another as members of society. Unfortunately, the social sciences are often referred to as "soft" sciences, which implies that they are not in the same league as the "hard" sciences that we hear so much about.

But the social sciences are not truly soft. Indeed, they are essential if we are to address and resolve the many problems that confront us — and not just matters such as drug abuse and crime, two areas of interest to social scientists. The way people live and work affects the earth, seas, and the sky. This relationship between people and their environment — indeed there is a complex interplay between society, science, and technology as well — must be understood if environmental problems such as greenhouse warming are to be solved. The number of people on this earth, the kind of lives they lead, and the tools they work with are what tie society to, and help ruin, nature.

If we do not consider what truly lies behind environmental degradation — notably the behavior and plight of society's members — then all attempts to clean up the planet will fail. More emphasis on science and technology is not going to do it, no more than simply hiring more police officers can eradicate crime. Science can help clean up the environment, just as more police can help lessen crime. But neither the police nor scientists can do their jobs alone. Both have to be part of a bigger plan that considers the social and economic problems that are to blame for the difficulties that must be resolved. An all-out attack on poverty and overpopulation is as important in the long run as the development of inventions that clean up the environment, make energy more efficient, and give us safer incinerators and waste dumps.

Once again, there is no single solution to our environmental crisis, nor is the cleanup of planet Earth the responsibility of a single group of specialists or a single nation.

11
THE PROBLEM:

ENERGY

Yes, energy is an environmental problem. Not the kind of energy that invigorates track stars, rock musicians, and everyone else who works hard at what they do. The type of energy that is an environmental problem is fuel, the kind of fuel that powers our cars and planes, runs our factories and furnaces, and lights our homes. That sort of energy comes from sources that are polluting the earth, air, and water with waste products.

Those sources are quite familiar to you by now: coal, oil, gas, wood, and nuclear fuel. Each one keeps the world humming, moving, heated, cooled, healthy, entertained, fed, and safe. But they have their dark, contaminating sides as well, as we have seen. From acid rain to nuclear fallout, pollution from the materials we burn to generate energy seems to be the price we must pay for making electricity for homes and industry and for satisfying the increasing need to drive and fly and dash over and under the waves more often and at ever faster speeds.

But does our thirst for energy have to mean the death of our environment? Are there better ways to use our current fuels? Are there other, cleaner fuels that will move us from one place to another and generate electricity? Let's examine the two most important uses of fuel: transportation and the generation of electric power.

TRANSPORTATION

Except when we go from here to there on foot, by bike, by sailboat, or by glider, we depend on fuel for transportation. Usually, that fuel is oil. Oil runs our cars and trains, ships and planes.

There are many kinds of oil, vegetable and animal oils among them, but for energy we are talking about petroleum. This is a naturally occurring mixture of hydrocarbons, which are organic compounds made of carbon and hydrogen. Organic substances are derived from living organisms, and in the case of petroleum the source is believed to be decayed plankton and other simple plants buried deep in the earth.

Ever since the first oil well was drilled in Pennsylvania in the 1800s, petroleum has played a very important role in running motor vehicles for just about everyone on earth. Oil is found in many places besides the United States: in the Middle East, including the Persian Gulf area, where two-thirds of the world's crude oil is located; the Soviet Union; Africa; Venezuela; and Mexico. No one knows for sure, but scientists believe that there are more huge reserves of petroleum under the ice of Antarctica.

How much oil is there in the ground? Again, no one can pinpoint the amount down to the exact barrel. But the estimate is around a trillion barrels, nearly three percent of which is in the United States.

That sounds like a lot of oil, and it is. Just think about how much we use of it: 24 barrels per person a year in the United States (we import 50 percent of our oil), and 12 barrels per person in Western Europe, for a worldwide average of 4.5 barrels a year per person![1] A lot of that oil is in the form of gasoline, which is refined from petroleum, and Americans consume it as though it were water: we represent only 4 percent of the earth's population, but we burn up some 40 percent of the gasoline.

Unfortunately, at the rate petroleum is being used it won't last forever. Not only will our reserves all be gone one day but they will not be replaced.

Obviously, if we are to make oil last as long as possible, we have to use it carefully. Also, as we know, careful burning protects the environment, and that is why petroleum scientists have come up with products such as reformulated, or "clean," gasoline, which does not evaporate as easily as ordinary gasoline and, thus, does not put as many pollutants into the air.

We have already started to cut back a bit on how much oil we use. In the U.S., for example, oil now produces only 5 percent of our electricity, compared to 17 percent fifteen years ago. While our car manufacturers could do far better, automobiles now average 27 miles per gallon, up from only 14 miles per gallon, saving 420,000 barrels of oil a day.[2]

But besides driving smaller, fuel-efficient cars, we can also conserve our vital oil supplies by driving less, by using car pools, and by using public transportation more. If we all heeded that advice, air pollution would be reduced by a surprisingly significant amount. Here's how Marcia Lowe, a senior researcher at the Worldwatch Institute, sees cities of the future that are not dominated by cars:

> The heart of the city would be reserved for people on foot and passengers arriving by metro or trolley. Beyond the core, pedestrians, cyclists, trolleys, and buses would share the streets equitably with slow car traffic. Express public transport routes would link outlying areas to each other and to downtown. People would make most short trips by foot or bike, and longer trips by walking or biking to public transport stops. Cars would be reserved for trips for which the alternatives are inconvenient.[3]

Lowe points out that around the world, even in countries that rely heavily on cars, governments and citizens are beginning to look at transportation somewhat differently. For example:

> • Nearly all major European cities have converted part of their centers to pedestrian zones.

• The mayor of Paris was apparently so impressed by how temporary parking restrictions for France's 1989 bicentennial reduced traffic that he announced plans to permanently remove more than 100,000 street parking spaces in central Paris to make room for public transport, cyclists, and pedestrians.

• Even California, a state with a strong "car culture" and the worst air pollution, has made a new commitment to public transportation in Los Angeles, San Diego, and San Jose.

• The city of Harare in the African nation of Zimbabwe now requires merchants to provide secure bike parking.

• Bicycles in Asia alone now outnumber the world's cars.[4]

Another way to conserve gasoline — one that may not be too popular — is to raise the cost of oil, place a heavy tax on new cars, or impose heavier gasoline taxes. Lowe points out that one of the surest ways to lessen overdependence on cars is to make drivers pay more for the true costs of automobile use, including municipal services and road construction and repair. Also, fewer than ten percent of employees pay for parking in the U.S., and employers can deduct from their taxes the costs of providing employee parking. Commuters who pay for their own parking are far more likely to carpool or take public transportation.[5]

But running our motor vehicles less, for all that it does to protect the environment and keep more oil in the bank, only postpones the day when we'll run out of gas. We need to develop substitutes. Two that scientists are examining are methanol and ethanol, which are forms of alcohol. Methanol is best obtained from natural gas, although it may be made from wood, coal, agricultural waste, or garbage; ethanol is made from wood and grain. Some sources say that these alternative fuels are more expensive than gasoline; some say they're cheaper. Such conclusions also depend, of course, on the fluctuating price of gas. These fuels are believed to be less polluting than gasoline, although environmentalists point out that burning any fuel can discharge pollutants into the air and that methanol may be a health hazard when it is handled by mechanics and pump attendants. Both alternative fuels are being used now and can be burned in existing cars if engines are altered somewhat; but new engines that are designed to burn only these fuels are being tested. Ethanol blended with gasoline — the mixture is called gasohol — is used in some U.S. cars, but in Brazil pure ethanol extracted from sugarcane runs about a third of the 13 million automobiles. Ethanol and methanol fuels still need to be studied to determine if they can truly compete with gasoline because they generally provide less energy per gallon than gasoline. There is also the question of how many trees would have to be cut down to make enough ethanol to go around, and whether there's enough grain in the world to both feed people and run motor vehicles.

Cars can also run on natural gas, or methane. There is plenty of it in North America (the U.S. and the Soviet Union have half the world's reserves), and it is already used as a vehicle fuel in Italy, Canada, and elsewhere. Natural gas is a relatively clean-burning fuel that produces fewer of the chemicals that cause smog. Existing engines can handle natural gas, but to run well they need to be modified, and engineers are working on this. There are, however, problems with natural gas as a car fuel. The gas does create nitrogen oxides, which can contribute to acid rain. Cars have to be fitted with cumbersome containers to hold the gas — and it is a true gaseous element, unlike the "gas" that is short for liquid gasoline. Also, many people, fearful of an explosion if the stuff leaks out, are wary of carrying bottled gas around with them.

There are a few other ways we might achieve car power without ruining the environment. One very promising one is the electric car. Because it runs on batteries, it is nonpolluting and doesn't waste precious fuel reserves. The electric car is not new. It came out in 1843, long before gasoline-driven cars appeared in the U.S., and soon was being used here and in Europe. Eventually, the gasoline engine caught on, and except for a few electric delivery vans, utility vehicles, and golf carts, Americans lost interest in electric automobiles.

Until now. Engineers have revived the idea of an electric car fleet, and a few new battery-operated cars and vans are rolling. Besides running cleanly, electric cars require few mechanical parts, are easy to operate, need little maintenance, and are dependable. But, again, there are drawbacks. Electric cars have to be recharged when their batteries run down. They cannot hit the high speeds gasoline-powered cars do — so far the test models' top speed is about 50 miles an hour — and they can travel only around 40 to 50 miles before the battery has to be recharged. As research progresses, it is expected that both speed and range will be improved. Some engineers believe that new batteries will double the range and boost the speed to around 70 miles an hour. Experimental cars fitted with solar cells that convert the energy from sunlight into electricity are also being tested, and if such a concept ever catches on it might be even better than a car whose battery must be charged by plugging it into a socket — if only because at the far end of that socket is the power plant that supplies electricity that still must be generated by coal, oil, or nuclear power.

Finally, we should mention another fuel with potential for automobiles: hydrogen. The simplest and lightest of the elements, hydrogen combines with oxygen to form water. In liquid form, hydrogen is used as a fuel in rocket engines, and the Soviet Union has developed an airplane that flies on liquid hydrogen. Some scientists believe the fuel can be used also to power our cars and trucks, and several experimental models have been tested. As an energy source, hydrogen is almost free of pollutants. It can be made from fossil fuels and from water, but it is very expensive to make. In cars, it would also require cumbersome fuel tanks, and at this moment a tankful cannot take a car very far.

What about trains? Can a kind of train be developed that runs without polluting the air as oil-burning diesel engines do? It's already been done. The electricity-driven, magnetically levitated train, called a maglev or a magtrain, is a spectacular invention that literally flies along, hovering above special tracks, at speeds as high as 300 miles an hour.

Like the electric car, electric trains are not new. Streetcars, subway trains, and commuter lines have long been operated by electricity. Maglev trains are an enormous improvement, and quite different.

They have large, special electromagnets, called superconducting magnets, arranged underneath their cars. More magnets are set in the floor and in the sides of a U-shaped aluminum guideway, a sort of trough that replaces tracks, over which the train passes. What keeps the train moving and flying over the trough is the repulsive force of magnets — the sort of thing that happens when you push two magnets together. As the magnetic field from the magnets on the bottom of the train meets the field from the magnets in the guideway, the train lifts up about four inches off the guideway. An engineer sitting in a control house at one end of the roadbed (there is no engineer aboard the train) sends electricity, which comes from a power plant, into the guideway magnets. As the electricity flows from one magnet to the other, the magnets alternately pull and push the train forward. It is somewhat like what happens when a surfer rides ashore on breaking waves, only with the magtrain the waves are magnetic.

Magtrains of different types are being tested in Japan and Germany, and they have many advantages. Because magtrains are suspended (they have wheels, but only for support when the train starts out), there is no contact between steel wheels and steel tracks, which in ordinary trains creates friction and limits speed. There are fewer mechanical parts, so there is less costly maintenance, and the trains are noiseless and move with little vibration. More important, magtrains can run on electrical energy provided by sources other than oil — coal, nuclear power, and hydroelectricity. The trains' unique magnetic design also reduces energy consumption, energy that, when all things are considered, is used by maglevs more efficiently than a car traveling the same distance.

The drawbacks? Critics say the special magnets required are not yet perfected for large-scale use (the test models run only a few miles), that the cost of building new tracks is too expensive for long-distance hauling, and that obtaining rights-of-way is difficult. There might also be parking nightmares as passengers flock to the lots at either end to catch 100-car trains that carry 100,000 passengers a day. Despite the critics, however, maglev research still goes on, and one day it could well provide us with a magic flying carpet.

Finally, we should mention ships because they are important in transportation and because they also pollute the air when they belch fumes from the oil or coal they use for fuel. Except for installing giant sails — which has actually been tried on some ships — there would appear to be little we can do to lessen ships' dependence on fossil fuels.

There is one thing we can do, though it smacks a bit of science fiction. It is the magship, a concept of ship propulsion that originated in the United States and has since been refined in Japan. Several test models, one of them around twelve feet long, have been operated successfully in tanks of water. While they don't move very fast — one traveled at only around a mile an hour — the striking thing about magships is that, unlike conventional ships, they have no motors and no moving parts at all.

In an ordinary ship, powerful engines fueled by diesel oil generate the power that turns screw propellers, which push the ship through the water. In the magship, superconducting magnets like the ones on the magtrain are arranged along the hull. The magnets beam strong magnetic fields into the water, and at the same time a generator on the ship sends an electric current into the water between electrodes that are also attached to the underside of the ship. The same principle of repulsion between magnets drives the ship: when the field from the magnets meets the electric current in the seawater, the two forces repel one another and the ship is shoved forward. The fuel, in effect, is the seawater, which, unlike fresh water, contains a rich concentration of dissolved salts that are excellent conductors of electricity.

If real magships are ever built — and some engineers believe that 100-ton vessels are sure to come — they would have some great advantages over conventional ships. Since they have no moving parts, the ships would be far easier to build and service. Like magtrains, magships move without vibration or noise, a particular advantage for military and research submarines, which depend on silence to do their work. Where an ordinary ship's propellers often waste energy when they race in rough weather as the stern moves in and out of the waves, a propless magship doesn't have any such problems: because it relies on the plentiful seawater for its power, it can produce an enormous amount of thrust in almost any kind of weather. Electromagnetic power would also be most valuable in an icebreaker ship because there would be no propellers or rudder to damage as the ship crunched its way through heavy ice. Finally, driving a magship would be incredibly easy — all the pilot would need would be a few buttons to control the current.

Are there drawbacks? Of course. Like the magtrain, the magnet technology required — superconducting magnets are in no way similar to those horseshoe-shaped magnets we are all familiar with — is not ready, at least not at the stage that would make a fleet of heavy magships economical. Critics also say that the ship's magnetic field might attract all sorts of metal debris, even larger objects such as other ships. The amount of salt in the water might also be an obstacle, and the powerful generators that pump electric current into the water could be too expensive to build. Still, magships, like magtrains and hydrogen-powered cars, may one day be moving future generations.

GENERATING ELECTRICITY

Electricity can be made by putting many different resources to work: oil, coal, radioactive elements, water, the sun, wind, or the heat that is trapped beneath the earth. Although some people still manage to live without electricity, the industrialized world would certainly be a far different place than it is today without it.

The challenge that faces everyone who provides us with electricity is, of course, how to make it without sending all those pollutants into the air, notably the ones that come from fossil fuels. Can it be done? What are the alternatives to oil, coal, and gas?

Insofar as oil is concerned, U.S. utilities generally burn around 600,000 barrels of oil a day, which amounts to about five percent of the fuel we use to generate electricity. (Parts of the country, such as New England and New York, obtain a third of their electricity from oil-powered plants.)

Coal is king when it comes to generating electricity, providing around 75 percent of our electric power, and nuclear energy is second, producing 20 percent. Because coal is so abundant and so important a source of power, it is easy to understand why we still burn so much of it.

But what of the acid rain, global climate change, lung diseases, and all the other concerns that are linked to coal? Certainly, coal can be used in ways that do not pollute the atmosphere as dangerously as in the past. The U.S. Department of Energy and a number of industries have spent billions of dollars in efforts to develop what are called clean coal technologies, and many demonstration projects are under way here and overseas.

Scrubbers, as we have seen, are already in use, and they do remove sulfur from smokestack gases. But they do not clear out other greenhouse gases, and they are expensive. That is why energy specialists are looking for new technology that would eliminate more pollutants from coal burning, as well as trying to develop new methods of trapping coal gases after they are released.

"If we shut down every single coal-fired utility in the country today," W. Henson Moore, the deputy secretary of energy, told a mining meeting in 1990,

> we'd wreak economic havoc, and all that disruption and chaos would not make an appreciable difference in the level of greenhouse gases. Shutting down every coal-fired utility in the United States would reduce greenhouse gases just three percent worldwide, not a very attractive cost-benefit ratio.[6]

In contrast, Moore pointed out, if we were to improve the efficiency of coal combustion, we would make sizable reductions in carbon dioxide emissions. Today's plants run at 33-percent efficiency, and boosting that to 45 percent would, according to Moore, reduce carbon dioxide emissions nearly 25 percent.

One piece of coal technology is called gasification. It involves drying raw coal and heating it to force gases out. The gases are cleaned and then cooled so that they can produce liquid fuel or be burned to generate electricity. The remaining solid fuel has a much higher heating value than raw coal, and it can also be used to generate electricity. "Our ability to produce clean liquid fuels from our own coal supplies strikes at the heart of those who would hold us hostage to imported oil," Robert Gentile, the Department of Energy's assistant secretary for fossil energy, observed recently. "And because these fuels are clean, we also show that coal use does not mean compromising our commitment to the environment."[7]

We cannot, of course, forget nuclear energy. Its advantages and disadvantages, as we have seen, are many. And it is being used widely, despite the arguments and the opposition. Many countries rely on it to generate their electricity far more than we do, even though we have more nuclear power plants on line than any other country: France and Belgium depend on nuclear plants for two-thirds of their electricity; Korea, for 53 percent; Taiwan, 48 percent; Sweden, 45 percent; Japan, Germany, and Spain, 31 percent.[8]

But the nuclear waste problem and the potential for danger stand in the way of even wider use. Nuclear power, like coal, is an exceptional source of energy, and it behooves scientists to work harder at making both sources safer and more acceptable to the public. We do, after all, need them both, and oil, too, and to stop using them before better, alternative methods of producing energy are developed would be irresponsible and foolish.

THE ALTERNATIVES

We've used the word *alternatives* a lot. Environmentalists use it a lot, especially when talking about the clean, renewable energy sources that could be solid options to fossil fuels. The renewable energy sources include solar energy, wind power, hydropower, tidal power, geothermal energy, biomass energy, and electrochemical fuel cells. Do they work? Can they reduce our dependence on fossil fuels?

Without doubt, they do work. But whether they will reduce our dependence on fossil fuels in the near future remains to be seen. One recent study by the Worldwatch Institute concludes that four decades from now, renewable energy resources could be supplying more than half the world's energy. Others are not so sure.

That the materials required to make the transition are available is a given. In the United States alone, the renewable energy waiting to be tapped in sunlight, wind, falling water, green plants, and the heated interior of the earth adds up to more than 200 times as much energy as our country now uses.[9]

Moreover, many of the alternative methods of generating heat and electricity are already in use. Waste-to-energy incinerators and the production of ethanol and methanol to run cars are examples of biomass energy; biomass energy today is the primary source of energy for nearly half of the world's population, some 2.5 billion people in developing countries. Hydropower, the generation of electricity using water power, is the source of about a fifth of the world's electricity. Geothermal energy, which uses underground heat, supplies 40 percent of the electricity in El Salvador and around 11 percent in Kenya. Wind power generates electricity through windmills, towers topped by propeller-driven mechanical turbines, which are placed in windy areas. This form of power provides electricity to many Californians; Denmark, the world's second largest wind energy producer after California, got about 2 percent of its power from windmills in 1990.[10]

You are probably more familiar with solar energy, the energy given off by the sun as electromagnetic radiation. Obtaining energy from the sun seems simple enough. Devices called photovoltaic cells — the same units that are found in pocket calculators and in camera light meters — convert the light radiation into electricity, and other devices called solar collectors gather the sun's rays as heat to make steam instead of electricity.

Solar energy is in relatively wide use, too. In the Middle East, solar energy heats the water in many homes, and more than a million solar heating systems have been built in the U.S. Thousands of Third World villages rely on solar cells for electricity. Large solar-power systems in California now generate power for as little as eight cents a kilowatt-hour — less than electricity from new nuclear plants.

Collecting the free sun's rays is not very difficult. All sorts of panels, tiles, dishes, shingles, and mirrors do that job quite well. But storing solar energy is difficult, and until that can be done easily, solar power will have a tough time becoming the world's main energy source. There are, however, many ways to store solar energy, among them batteries. Also, scientists can use photovoltaic cells to split water molecules into hydrogen and oxygen, a process which absorbs electrical energy. The hydrogen can be stored and transported through pipelines like natural gas and burned when required. It can also be recombined in fuel cells with the oxygen to generate electricity without burning. Fuel cells are the powerful devices that provided the electricity for the *Apollo* astronauts who went to the moon.

Finally, there's wave power — using the power of tides to generate electricity. For years, scientists have dreamed of harnessing the enormous energy in parts of the world where tides run high. Various plans would trap incoming high tidewater, run it through turbines to generate electricity, then let it wash back out to sea at low tide. Although the process has great potential, given the huge amounts of electricity that could be generated and the many places where tides are perfect for the job, it appears to be enormously expensive.

Again, will these alternative sources of energy reduce our dependence on fossil fuels? They probably will one day — and indeed, they must. As fossil fuels run out on us, we have to take steps now. Because a sudden shift from a conventional form of power to an unconventional one is highly unlikely, we should be thinking about alternatives now, not later on when the wells and the mines are dry. For those of you who want a career in public service, there will be endless opportunities to propose alternatives and to see that they are put into effect. For those of you who want a career in science, there are also great opportunities to develop imaginative alternatives.

No one can say which of the energy alternatives, or which combination, will supply the world's needs in the future. But perhaps, just perhaps, we will one day get all the energy we require by tapping the power that lies in and beneath the water that covers the earth. Fusion, wave power, hydrogen for our cars, the vast reservoir of solar heat that is stored in the ocean, hydroelectric plants, the salty fuel for magships — each is a marvelous alternative to fossil fuels, which, for all their power, are in limited supply and are crude in comparison to what imaginative science can do.

Perhaps the words of the prophetic Jules Verne should be heeded. In 1874, he wrote in his book, *The Mysterious Island:*

I believe that water will one day be employed as fuel, that hydrogen and oxygen which constitute it, used singly or together, will furnish an inexhaustible source of heat and light.

Whether the future of energy lies there, it is in your hands.

NOTES

INTRODUCTION

1. Clyde Haberman, "Pope Harshly Rebukes Lands That Foster Ecological Crisis," *New York Times* (December 6, 1988) p. 16.

1 • TOO MANY CHEMICALS

1. Philip Shabecoff, "Apple Sales Rise After Scare of '89," *New York Times* (October 13, 1990) p. A28.
2. "No Evidence of Asbestos Danger in Schools," *New Scientist* (January 27, 1990) p. 26.
3. "Brazil Enlists DDT Against Mosquito Outbreak," *Worldwatch* (July–August 1990) p. 9.
4. Ibid., p. 10.
5. Dixie Farley, "Chemicals We'd Rather Dine Without," *FDA Consumer* (September 1988) p. 15.
6. Timothy Egan, "Some Say Mining Company's Move Could Thwart U.S. Plan for Cleanup," *New York Times* (October 2, 1990) p. A20.
7. "Japanese Justice Fails Mercury Victims," *New Scientist* (October 13, 1990) p. 12.
8. Farley, "Chemicals We'd Rather Dine Without," p. 13.
9. J. P. deGarbino, "Do We Really Need All These Chemicals?" *World Health* (January-February 1990) p. 14.

2 • TOO MUCH NOISE

1. Allan R. Gold, "A Manhattan Skyscraper Is Told to Stop Whistling," *New York Times* (December 7, 1990) p. 1.
2. *The American Medical Association Family Medical Guide* (New York: Random House, 1982) p. 339.
3. J. H. Cushman, Jr., "Accord Reached on Ridding Skies of Noisy Planes," *New York Times* (October 27, 1990) p. 1.
4. "Quality of the Environment in Japan," Japan Environmental Agency (1980) p. 12.

3 • BAD AIR

1. "The Crucial Decade: The 1990s and the Global Environmental Challenge," World Resources Institute (January 1989) p. 11.
2. "The State of the World Population," United Nations Population Fund (1990) p. 9.
3. "Air Pollution Now Threatening Health Worldwide," Worldwatch Institute news release (May 12, 1990).
4. "A Critical Balance," United Nations Population Fund news release (1990).
5. "Clearing the Air: A Global Agenda," Worldwatch Paper 94, Worldwatch Institute (1990) p. 5.
6. "Teens Who Smoke," American Academy of Pediatrics fact sheet (December 1990).
7. "Our Planet, Our Health," World

Health Organization fact sheet (April 7, 1990).

8. "Clearing the Air," p. 9.

9. "Plant Said to Foul Grand Canyon Air," *New York Times* (October 16, 1990) p. A24.

10. Charles Seabrook, "Breathing: The Latest Hazard to the Nation's Health," in the series "Ill Winds," *Atlanta Constitution* (July 9–15, 1989) published in pamphlet form, p. 13.

11. Bill Keller, "In Polluted Russian City a New Fear," *New York Times* (November 26, 1990) p. A8.

12. Robert Hanley, "New Jersey Fear of Toxic Metal Rises After Tests," *New York Times* (August 24, 1989) p. B2.

13. "Biomass Burning Ignites Concern," *Science News* (March 31, 1990) p. 196.

14. "Our Planet, Our Health."

15. Philip Shabecoff, "Acid Rain Report Confirms Concern," *New York Times* (September 6, 1990) p. A24.

16. "Ozone Destruction Closer to Home," *Science* (March 16, 1990) p. 1297.

17. Ibid.

18. Philip Shabecoff, "9% Decline in Toxic Pollution Is Cited in EPA Survey," *New York Times* (April 20, 1990) p. A11.

19. Seabrook, "Breathing: The Latest Hazard," p. 14.

4 • DYING WATER

1. "America's Clean Water Act," America's Clean Water Foundation (1990).

2. Ibid.

3. "Venice Turns the Tide on Its Polluted Lagoon," *New Scientist* (February 3, 1990) p. 29.

4. D. R. Kester, "Marine Pollution: Winning or Losing?" *Maritimes,* University of Rhode Island Graduate School of Oceanography (May 1989) pp. 1–2.

5. "Explore All Options for Solving Irrigation-Induced Water-Quality Problems," National Resources Council news release (October 17, 1989).

6. Ibid.

7. "Less Ozone Means More Ultraviolet; Ocean Life Could Suffer," American Chemical Society news release (September 13, 1989).

8. Clare Collins, "Old Oil Tanks Threaten Water," *New York Times* (April 1, 1990) p. 20.

9. "Drinking Water." *Renew America* (February 1989) p. 19.

10. "Drinking Water Protection," *Renew America* (1990) p. 19.

11. Philip Shenon, "Despite Laws, Water in Schools May Contain Lead," *New York Times* (October 31, 1990) p. 1.

12. S. Koppes, "Streams Can Serve as an Early Warning System," *ASU Research,* Arizona State University (Winter 1990) p. 17.

13. Trevor Davis, "As Pure As the Driven Snow?" *New Scientist* (April 8, 1989) p. 45.

14. "Coalition Urges Action to Save U.S. Wetlands," *New York Times* (November 15, 1989) p. A18.

15. Jeff Hecht, "The Incredible Shrinking Mississippi Delta," *New Scientist* (April 14, 1990) p. 35.

16. "America's Clean Water Act."

17. Worldwatch Institute, *State of the World, 1990* (New York: W. W. Norton, 1990) p. 46.

18. "Drinking Water Protection," *Renew America* (1990) pp. 19–20.

19. "Safeguarding the Future," World Health Organization news release (1990).

20. Sandy Cairncross, "Water!" *World Health* (February 1990) p. 23.

5 • TOO MUCH WASTE

1. "Public Attitudes Toward Garbage Disposal," National Solid Wastes Management Association (May 4, 1989) p. 2.
2. "Solid Waste Recycling," *Renew America* (February 1989) p. 12.
3. Nicholas Freudenberg, "Not in Our Backyards," *Monthly Review Press* (1984) p. 31.
4. *The Problem of Waste Disposal* (Bronx, New York: H. W. Wilson Company, 1989) p. 115.
5. "Medical Waste Management," National Solid Wastes Management Association (1989) p. 1.
6. Ibid.
7. Earth Works Project, *Fifty Simple Things You Can Do to Save the Earth* (Alahambra, CA: Green Leaf Press, 1989) p. 44.
8. C. P. Shea, "Doing Well By Doing Good," *Worldwatch* (November-December 1989) p. 20.
9. Worldwatch Institute, *State of the World, 1988* (New York: W. W. Norton, 1988) p. 132.
10. Ibid.
11. Timothy Egan, "Some Say Mining Company's Move Could Thwart U.S. Plan for Cleanup," *New York Times* (October 2, 1990) p. A20.
12. Earth Works, *Fifty Simple Things*, p. 67.
13. "U.S. Garbage Disposal Needs Could Exceed Existing Landfill Capacity by 1998," National Solid Wastes Management Association news release (May 4, 1989).
14. Associated Press, "Trash Haulers Get 12-Year Terms for Illegal Dumping," *New York Times* (October 5, 1990) p. B3.
15. *Health and Environment Digest* (September-October 1989), p. 13.
16. William E. Schmidt, "Trying to Solve the Side Effects of Converting Trash to Energy," *New York Times* (May 27, 1990) p. E5.
17. Allen Hershkowitz, "Burning Trash: How It Could Work," *Technology Review* (July 26, 1987) p. 34.
18. Jeff Hecht, "Sunlight Gives Toxic Waste a Tanning," *New Scientist* (April 14, 1990) p. 28.
19. "Solid Waste Reduction," *Renew America* (1990) p. 50.
20. Ibid.
21. H. A. Walker and J. F. Paul, "Ocean Dumping of Sewage Sludge," *Maritimes*, University of Rhode Island Graduate School of Oceanography (May 1989) p. 15.
22. Ibid.
23. K. R. Hinga and J. A. Knauss, "Ocean Disposal: Some Aspects of the Debate," *Maritimes*, University of Rhode Island Graduate School of Oceanography (May 1989) p. 8.
24. Ibid., p. 9.
25. John Langone, "A Stinking Mess," *Time* (January 2, 1989) p. 21.
26. "Environmental Refugees: A Yardstick of Habitability." Worldwatch Paper 86, Worldwatch Institute (November 1986) p. 27.
27. Langone, "A Stinking Mess," p. 22.
28. Ibid., p. 23.
29. Priscilla Painton, "Greening from the Roots Up," *Time* (April 23, 1990) p. 83.

6 • RADIATION POLLUTION

1. Felicity Barringer, "Four Years Later,

Soviets Reveal Wider Scope to Cherno-byl Horror," *New York Times* (April 28, 1990) p. 1.

2. "The Colorless, Odorless Killer," *Time* (July 22, 1985) p. 72.

3. Jacob Kastner, "The Natural Radiation Environment." In *Understanding the Atom*, U.S. Atomic Energy Commission (1968) p. 5.

4. Zhores Medvedev, *The Legacy of Chernobyl* (New York, W. W. Norton, 1990) pp. 133–34.

5. Philip Elmer-Dewitt, "Nuclear Power Plots a Comeback," *Time* (February 2, 1989) p. 19.

6. Stansfield Turner and Thomas Davies, "Plutonium Terror on the High Seas," *New York Times* (April 28, 1990) p. 25.

7 • TOO MUCH HEAT

1. Michael Lemonick, "Feeling the Heat," *Time* (January 2, 1989) p. 16.

2. *EPRI Journal* (June 1988) p. 10.

3. Ibid., p. 11.

4. "Methane: The Hidden Greenhouse Gas," *New Scientist* (May 6, 1989) p. 37.

5. "Our Planet, Our Health," World Health Organization fact sheet (April 7, 1990).

6. Worldwatch Institute. *State of the World, 1990* (New York: W. W. Norton, 1990) p. 17.

7. "The Greenhouse Effect: Hardly Apocalypse," *New York Times* (August 23, 1990) p. A24.

8. "Greenhouse Skeptic out in the Cold," *Science* (December 1, 1989) p. 1118.

9. "Carbon Dioxide Warming Is Good for the Planet," *New York Times* (May 7, 1990) p. A14.

8 • DEFORESTATION

1. Peter Steinhart, "Replanting the Forest," *Audubon* (March 1990) p. 26.

2. Rushworth M. Kidder, "When the Rainforests Go," *Christian Science Monitor* (August 7, 1986) p. 10.

3. Charles Seabrook, "Brazil's March Westward Topples Lush Forests," in the series "Ill Winds," *Atlanta Constitution*, (July 9–15, 1989) published in pamphlet form, p. 29.

4. Catherine Caulfield, "Rare Rain Forests in U.S. Dying," *San Francisco Examiner* (May 21, 1986) p. 20.

5. "How Your Tax Dollars Kill the Rainforests," Rainforest Action Network advertisement, *New York Times* (October 16, 1990) p. 7.

6. Steinhart, "Replanting the Forest."

7. "Oregon's Ancient Laboratory," *Worldwatch* (November-December 1990) p. 7.

9 • THREATENED WILDLIFE

1. Eugene Linden, "The Death of Birth," *Time* (January 2, 1989) p. 11.

2. John Langone, "Emerging Viruses," *Discover* (December 1990) p. 65.

3. Takashi Atoda, "Anti-Japan Sentiments Are at the Root of the Ban-Whaling Controversy," reprinted in *In Defense of Whaling*, Japanese Whaling Association (1981) p. 17.

4. "From Minnow to Sturgeon, North American Fish Are in Peril," *New York Times* (January 30, 1990) p. C4.

5. Anastasia Toufexis, "The Dirty Seas," *Time* (August 1, 1988) p. 47.

6. R. Haebler, "Environmental Contamination of the Oceans: Effects on Marine Mammals," *Maritimes*, University of Rhode Island Graduate School of Oceanography (May 1989) p. 6.

7. Norman Meyers, "The Mega-Extinction of Animals and Plants." In *Ecology 2000*, edited by Sir Edmund Hillary (New York: Beaufort Books, 1984) p. 86.

8. *World Atlas of Birds* (New York: Random House, 1974) p. 27.

9. Clarence J. Hylander, *Wildlife Communities* (Boston: Houghton Mifflin, 1966) p. 10. Steve Koppes, "Learning to Like Lichens," *ASU Research*, Arizona State University (Fall 1990) p. 14.

10. Koppes, "Learning to Like Lichens."

11. "Ignoring Pleas of Environmentalists, a Kansan Plows His Virgin Prairie," *New York Times* (November 23, 1990) p. B18.

12. Linden, "The Death of Birth," p. 13.

13. "Preserving Earth's Green Mantle," *Harvard Gazette* (April 20, 1990) p. 9.

14. Paul R. Ehrlich, *The Machinery of Nature* (New York: Simon and Schuster, 1986) p. 12.

15. Ibid.

16. "Chemists' Return to Nature Helps Farmers," *What's Happening in Chemistry?* American Chemical Society (1981) p. 25.

17. Ibid.

18. "Weapons Proliferate in War Against Insects," *What's New in Chemistry?* American Chemical Society (1988) p. 13.

19. Linden, "The Death of Birth," p. 13.

20. "America's Clean Water Act," America's Clean Water Foundation (1990).

21. Lewis Thomas, *The Lives of a Cell* (New York: Bantam Books, 1974) p. 170.

10 • POVERTY AND OVERPOPULATION

1. Anastasia Toufexis, "Too Many Mouths," *Time* (January 2, 1989) p. 24.

2. "Poverty Increased Worldwide During 1980s," Worldwatch Institute news release (March 10, 1990).

3. "Poverty and the Environment: Reversing the Downward Spiral," Worldwatch Paper 92, Worldwatch Institute (November 1989) p. 5.

4. Ibid., p. 49.

5. "Too Much Life on Earth," *New Scientist* (May 19, 1990) p. 28.

6. "Poverty and the Environment," p. 52.

7. B. B. Torrey and W. W. Kingkade, "Population Dynamics of the U.S. and the Soviet Union," *Science* (March 30, 1990) p. 1549.

8. Ann-Marie Dourien-Rollier, "Family Planning and the Law," *World Health* (April 1989) p. 7.

9. Selena Tenterden, "Induced Abortion: A World Review." In *Developing World Health* (Grosvenor Press International, 1988) p. 230.

10. Alan Durning, "Life on the Brink," *Worldwatch* (March-April 1990) pp. 27–28.

11. Toufexis, "Too Many Mouths."

11 • ENERGY

1. "Beyond the Petroleum Age: Designing a Solar Economy," Worldwatch Paper 100, Worldwatch Institute (December 1990) p. 12.

2. "The Penultimate Crisis." *Commonweal* (October 12, 1990) p. 563.

3. "The Urban Vehicle of the Future Is not the Car," Worldwatch Institute news release (October 13, 1990).

4. Ibid.

5. Ibid.

6. W. Henson Moore, U.S. Department of Energy, remarks before the American Mining Congress (May 7, 1990).

7. "Construction Begins for New Plant That Will Produce Clean, High Quality Fuels from Abundant U.S. Coal Supplies," U.S. Department of Energy news release (October 26, 1990).

8. "Electricity from Nuclear Engineering," U.S. Council for Energy Awareness (1989) p. 4.

9. "Solar Economy Dawning," Worldwatch Institute news release (December 15, 1990).

10. "Beyond the Petroleum Age," p. 23.

AN ENVIRONMENTAL GLOSSARY

Following are definitions of some key environmental words and terms. The names of specific chemicals and other substances that have a worrisome effect on the environment are treated in a separate list in chapter 1.

ACCLIMATIZATION. The process by which a living thing adjusts in order to survive when conditions change.

AEROSOL. A suspension of tiny solid or liquid particles in a gas. Smoke, fog, and clouds are aerosols, as are what's inside cans of hair spray, insecticide, and deodorant.

AIR POLLUTION. Contamination of the air by such things as aerosols, waste from smokestacks, crop spraying, and nuclear explosions.

ALGAE. Members of a large group of plants, many of them microscopic in size, that live largely in the water and are extremely important to the food chain, the feeding system that maintains life.

AQUIFER. Underground space in layers of rock, sand, and gravel in which water collects.

ATMOSPHERE. The air that surrounds the earth.

AUTOMOBILE EMISSION CONTROL. A method of reducing air pollution by removing certain ingredients from gasoline and by changing the design of automobile engines.

BALANCE OF NATURE. The way living things maintain their numbers in relationship to one another; the interaction between plants and animals that helps keep all life functioning smoothly.

BIODEGRADABLE. Capable of being broken down into a harmless substance by the action of microorganisms.

BIODIVERSITY. The variety of forms of plant and animal life.

BIOHAZARD. A substance that is hazardous to life.

BIOMASS. Plant materials and animal waste used as a source of fuel.

BIOSPHERE. The entire world of living things and the inanimate environment in which they live.

BIOTA. Plant and animal life.

BOTTOM ASH. Ash that remains at the bottom of an incinerator after waste is burned.

CHLOROPHYLL. Green pigment found in plants that absorbs light and changes it into chemical energy. (*See* photosynthesis.)

COMPOST. A mixture of decayed organic material used to fertilize and condition soil.

CONSERVATION. Preservation of the environment.

DEFORESTATION. The clearing out of forests.

DESERTIFICATION. The process by which a piece of land is transformed into a desert.

ECOLOGY. The study of how all living things, both plants and animals, relate to their natural environment.

ECOSYSTEM. A subdivision of the biosphere, a special community of life-forms working together and with their environment. Ponds, forests, and deserts are examples of ecosystems.

ENDANGERED SPECIES. Animals and plants in danger of extinction.

ENVIRONMENT. The surroundings in which plants and animals live.

EROSION. The wearing away of the earth's surface, as by water, glaciers, and wind.

EUTROPHICATION. A concentration of fertilizers and other plant nutrients in water that leads to explosive growth of algae and other plants and a loss of oxygen in the water.

EXTINCTION. Disappearance from the earth of species of plants or animals.

FALLOUT. Radioactive particles that have dropped on the earth from the atmosphere.

FERTILIZERS. Materials that are added to the soil to provide the necessary food for plant growth.

FLY ASH. Pollutant-containing ash that pours out of waste-incinerator smoke-stacks.

FOOD CHAIN. The movement of food energy from smaller organisms to larger ones when one kind of life-form consumes another.

FOSSIL FUEL. The remains of dead and decayed plant and animal life, which can take the form of coal, oil, or natural gas and which can be burned to produce energy.

FUNGICIDE. A substance that kills fungi, members of a group of parasitic plants that includes molds, mildews, and mushrooms.

GAIA. A theory, named after the Greek goddess of the earth, that suggests that the whole world acts as a single organism.

GLOBAL WARMING. A heating up of the earth caused by the discharge of gases from cars and factories into the atmosphere.

GRASSLANDS. Places without enough rainfall to produce vegetation other than grass.

GREENHOUSE EFFECT. Global warming as the result of a buildup of carbon dioxide and other greenhouse gases in the atmosphere.

GROUNDWATER. Water that has collected beneath the earth's surface in various spaces and cracks.

HABITATS. Any of the places on earth that support particular plants and animals.

HAZARDOUS WASTE. Any waste material — such as chemicals, incinerator ash, and medical trash — that exposes us to a health risk.

HERBICIDE. A substance used to kill unwanted plants.

HERBIVORES. Animals that feed only on plants.

HUMAN ECOLOGY. The study of the relation between human beings and their environment.

HYDROSPHERE. The waters of the earth.

INSECTICIDE. A chemical that kills insects.

IRRADIATION. Exposure to radiation.

LANDFILL. A waste dump.

LAND RECLAMATION. The process of

making useless land valuable and productive by irrigation, drainage, and fertilization.

LEACHATE. An often toxic "soup" of water and decomposed waste that may be released into groundwater.

MARSH. An area of soft, wet land, usually temporary.

MASS EXTINCTION. The abrupt disappearance from the earth of large numbers of species, as happened with the dinosaurs.

MUTATION. A sudden and permanent change in the hereditary material in a living cell.

NATURAL RESOURCE. A material supplied by nature that we can use, such as water, oil, minerals, and wood.

NIMBY. Initials standing for *Not in My Backyard.* Used to describe those who protest the location of a landfill, hazardous waste dump, or incinerator in their neighborhood.

NOISE. Unwanted sound, one of our environmental pollutants.

NUCLEAR ENERGY. Atomic energy, energy released from an atom's nucleus during a nuclear reaction in a nuclear power plant reactor or in an atomic bomb.

OCEAN DUMPING. The practice of disposing of garbage and other waste at sea.

OIL SPILL. The accidental release of oil from a seagoing tanker or during offshore drilling operations.

OZONE LAYER. An envelope of oxygenlike gas that surrounds the earth and protects us from the harmful ultraviolet rays of the sun.

PERMAFROST. Permanently frozen ground, as in Siberia and the polar regions.

PESTICIDE. A substance used to kill pesty plants and animals. Insecticides are also called pesticides.

PETROCHEMICALS. Chemicals made from petroleum and natural gas that are used to make plastics and detergents, among other products.

PHOTOSYNTHESIS. The process by which green plants convert sunlight into chemical energy and oxygen.

PHYTOPLANKTON. Tiny plants, mostly algae, that live in the sea and are a basic component of the food chain; phytoplankton are known as the grass of the sea. They are eaten by minuscule animals called zooplankton, which are the eggs and larvae of other small animals.

PLANKTON. Microscopic plants and animals that live in the sea. Most plankton is phytoplankton.

PLASTICS. A general term for natural and artificially made materials that can be molded into various shapes.

POLLUTION. Contamination or disruption of the environment by chemicals, smoke, nuclear radiation, noise, heat, or light.

RADIOACTIVITY. The ability of some elements, such as uranium, to emit various rays.

RAIN FOREST. A dense jungle found in the tropics where it rains regularly and there is no dry season.

RECYCLING. The recovery and reuse of waste materials.

RENEWABLE RESOURCE. A natural resource that is unlimited, such as energy from the sun or from water.

SALINIZATION. The depositing of crop-damaging salt when water evaporates in a dry area.

SAVANNA. Tropical grasslands in Africa and South America.

SMOG. A mixture of smoke and fog.

SOIL EROSION. The wearing away of soil, the topmost layer of the earth's surface.

SWAMP. A low-lying area of land that is covered with water, usually permanently.

TUNDRA. A treeless plain covered with moss and black mucky soil, with permafrost below; found in the arctic regions.

ULTRAVIOLET RADIATION. Energy produced by the sun or manufactured commercially for use in fluorescent lighting tubes and equipment to kill germs.

WASTE. Everything we throw away; goes by many names, including trash, refuse, garbage, sludge, or incinerator ash.

WASTE STREAM. All of the waste produced by a home or an industry.

WETLANDS. Marshes, swamps, bogs; essential ecosystems.

INDEX

Abbey, Henry, 116
acclimation, 128, 129
acetone, 63
acid flush, 46–47
acid rain, 2, 78
   from air pollution, 22, 29, 32, 33,
      34, 167, 176
   and destruction of forests, 3
   effects on fish, 136
   effects on water, 37
adaptation, 128, 129
aerosols, 14, 46
Agent Orange, 8–9, 12, 16
air pollution, 28–36
   from automobiles, 19–20, 169–172
   from biomass burning, 31–33
   from chemicals, 29
   from cigarettes, 22, 30
   and Clean Air Act, 35
   from generating energy, 167, 175,
      176
   from ozone, 32
   from pesticides, 30
   from radiation, 91, 92
   from ships, 174
   from waste incineration, 66–67, 76–
      78
Alar, 9–10
algal blooms, 42, 136, 137
American Forestry Association, 122
America's Clean Water Foundation,
     54–55
aquifers, 38–39, 49
Argonne National Laboratory, 70
Army Corps of Engineers, 48
arsenic, 10–11, 42, 58

asbestos, 11–12, 74
ash, 76–78
automobiles
   and air pollution, 19–20, 31, 35,
      169–172
   electric, 171–172
   and oil consumption, 169–172
   as source of waste, 61–62

bacteria, 42, 44, 52
batteries, 69, 77
Belokon', Dr. Valentin, 101–102
benzene, 65
Bhopal, India, 2, 29, 155
biodiversity, 128
biomass burning, 31–33
biomass energy, 177–178
birds
   and effects of DDT, 140–141
   and Styrofoam, 66
birth control. *See* family planning
Brazil
   and deforestation, 118–120, 124
Bullard, Robert, 76

cadmium, 61, 67, 68, 77, 136
cancer
   from air pollution, 30
   from asbestos, 12
   from chemical causes, 8, 10, 16, 21,
     65, 67
   from contaminated water supplies,
     46
   from food additives, 6, 22
   from hazardous waste, 58, 59
   from radiation, 34, 92–93, 96–99

carbon dioxide, 13, 176.
  See also greenhouse effect:
    greenhouse gases
carbon monoxide, 13, 35
Carson, Rachel, 6
cellophane, 64, 69
Center for Marine Conservation,
  60
CFCs, 13–14, 34–35, 66, 151.
  See also greenhouse effect:
    greenhouse gases
chemicals, 5–24
  and air pollution, 29
  cancer-causing in dumps, 58–59
  good uses for, 5–8
  petrochemicals, 57
  safe disposal of, 23–24
  toxic, 8–22, 69. *See also under*
    specific chemical names
  in water, 37–38, 40, 41
Chernobyl, 2, 91–93, 101, 151
chlorine, 13, 31, 45–46, 57, 68
chlorophyll, 43–45
chromium 31, 58
cigarettes, 22, 30
Clean Air Act, 35, 114
Clean Water Act, 50
Cleo Wrap of Tennessee, 69
climate, 1, 14, 176
coal, 102
  gasification of, 176–177
  role in air pollution, 30–31, 175–
    177.
  See also fossil fuels
composting, 57, 82
crustaceans, 137–138
Curie, Marie and Pierre, 99

daminozide. *See* Alar
DDT, 13, 14–15, 42
  effects on plants and wildlife, 14–15,
    136, 140–141, 146
decibel scale, 26
deforestation, 3, 110, 116–125, 146

conservation and management
    programs, 122, 125
  and the greenhouse effect, 114
  and logging, 121–124
  of rain forests, 117–121
  and poverty and overpopulation,
    153, 155
desalination, 53
desertification, 155
deuterium, 103
diatomaceous earth, 149
Dickens, Charles, 28, 30
dioxin, 8, 13, 16–17, 57, 77
diseases, 45–46, 137
DNA, 7
dolphins, 134–135
dredging and draining, 46, 47, 49
dumps. *See* landfills
Duphar Company, 69
Du Pont Company, 6
Durning, Alan, 152, 155–156

Earth Works Group, 73
ecological equilibrium, 40–41
ecosystems, 45, 131, 150
Ehrlich, Paul R., 147
electricity
  alternative methods for generating,
    177–180
  from coal, 175–176
  and emission of greenhouse gases,
    110
  and enviromental problems, 167–
    170
  from oil, 169
  from recycled waste, 80–81
electrochemical fuel cells, 177, 178
electromagnetic radiation. *See* solar
    energy
electromagnetic waves, 98
elephants, 138–139
El-Sayed, Dr. Sayed Z., 45
endangered species, 48, 120, 126–
    127

Act of 1973, 149–150
and overhunting, 138–139.
See also wildlife
energy resources, 1, 167–180
Environmental Defense Fund, 77
ethanol, 170
extinction of wildlife, 126–129, 143
by deforestation, 118–120
by habitat destruction, 139–140
by human acts, 126–129
Exxon *Valdez*, 129, 136

family planning
abortion, 157, 158, 160–166
contraception, 158–159, 163–164,
166
infanticide, 158–159, 164
sterilization, 158–160
fertilizers, 20, 42, 46, 57
and algal blooms, 136
control of, 150
and marine pollution, 44, 132
fish
and acid rain, 136
and offshore drilling of oil, 51
and polluted meltwater, 47
toxic chemicals in, 16–17, 21,
136
fission, 100–103
Flavin, Christopher, 112
food
additives, 6, 22
chain, 43–44, 130
effects of air pollution on, 29
PCBs in, 21
radiation in, 95, 96
forests, 144
conservation and management of,
124–125
and deforestation, 121–125
effects of acid rain on, 33.
See also rain forests
fossil fuels, 29, 35, 92, 102, 114
alternatives to, 170–171, 177–180

and emission of greenhouse gases,
110, 114, 115
fuel oil, 75, 167–175
gasoline, 75, 169–171
fusion, 102–103, 179

Gaia, 130
garbage and sewage, 2, 80.
See also waste; waste disposal
gasohol, 171
gasoline, 75, 169–170
substitutes for, 170–171
Gentile, Robert, 177
Georges Bank fishing grounds, 136
geothermal energy, 177–178
glaciers, 109, 112
global warming. *See* greenhouse effect
greenhouse effect, 3, 107–115
and animal migration, 131
greenhouse gases, 107–110, 176
and poverty and overpopulation,
154–155
and rain forests, 110
solutions to, 114–115
warnings and predictions about,
111–113

habitats, 139–140, 149–150
Haebler, Dr. Romona, 137
Hawaii, 118, 120
health hazards
from air pollution, 30, 32–33, 176
from asbestos, 11–12
from biomass burning, 32–33
from coal burning, 176
from dumping of toxic waste, 31,
58–62
from loud noises, 26–27
from methanol, 170–171
from ozone, 20
from radiation, 91–93, 96–99, 101–
102
from toxic chemicals, 10–11, 16–18
in water supplies, 45–46

herbicides, 10–11, 41, 143
  Agent Orange, 8–9
  dioxin, 16
  and viruses, 132
Hooker Chemical Company, 58–60
Hyatt, John Wesley, 64
hydrocarbons, 29, 31, 32, 35, 42
hydroelectric power, 39, 177–179
hydrogen, 172, 179
hydrogen chloride, 77
Hylander, Clarence J., 144

Ice Ages, 109
IGRs (insect growth regulators), 148
incinerators, 17–18, 76–78
Indonesia
  and deforestation, 118, 120–121
insecticides. *See* pesticides
insects, 3, 141–144
interdependency, 130
interrelationship, 130–131
irrigation, 42–43, 51
ivory, 138–139

Japan, 27
  recycling in, 81
  and whale hunting, 133
John Paul II, Pope, 1
Joliot-Curie, Irène, 99

Kesterton National Wildlife Refuge, 43
Knoll, Andrew, 146
Kubo, Dr. Isao, 148

landfills, 21, 58, 73–78, 81.
  See also waste; waste disposal
leachate, 57, 75
lead, 17–18, 68
  in air, 35
  in fish, 136
  in fly ash, 77
  in our bodies, 8, 18
  in waste disposal, 58

in water supplies, 46
Lindzen, Richard, 113
logging, 121–124, 140
Love Canal, 58–59, 61, 72–73
Lovelock, James, 130
Lowe, Marcia, 169–170
lung disease, 11–12, 32–33

McDonald's Corporation, 68
Maddox, John, 113
magnet technology, 173–175
manatees, 137
Medical Waste Policy Committee, 60
Mendes, Francisco, 118–119
mercury, 18–19
  in batteries, 68
  in cosmetics, 63
  danger to life, 6
  in fish, 136
  in landfills, 61
  in our bodies, 8
methane, 81.
  See also greenhouse effect:
    greenhouse gases
methanol, 170–171
Minamata disease, 19
Minnesota Mining and Manufacturing
    Company (3M), 69
Morgenthau, Hans, 113
Morris, G. P., 117
Morse, Dr. Stephen, 131–132
mosquitoes and DDT, 15
Müller, Paul, 14
Mysterious Island, The, 179–180

National Research Council, 31, 42
natural gas, 170–171
Nature, 113
nitrogen, 20
  nitrates, 42
  nitrogen dioxide, 19–20
  nitrogen oxide, 29, 33, 35, 46.

See also greenhouse effect:
    greenhouse gases
noise pollution, 25–27
nondegradable packaging, 82
nuclear fallout, 167
nuclear power, 92–93, 100–102, 177

offshore drilling, 49, 51
oil. *See* fossil fuels
oil spills, 2, 37, 84, 129
ozone
    as air pollutant, 20, 32, 33
ozone layer
    depletion of, 14, 33–35, 44–45, 107,
        156

parasites, 42
PCBs, 13, 21
    and destruction of plants, 146
    in dolphins, 135–137
    as marine pollutants, 42
"Peace with God the Creator, Peace
    with All of Creation," 1
Pelicano, 88–89
pesticides, 2, 6, 23–24, 41, 69
    in the atmosphere, 30
    control of, 147–150
    dioxin, 16
    and killing of birds, 140–141
    and lead, 17
    less dangerous types, 51
    use on insects, 5, 10–11, 143
petrochemicals, 57, 64
petroleum. *See* fossil fuels: fuel oil
pheromones, 149
phosphates, 42
photosynthesis, 44, 130
plankton, 44–45
plants, 3, 43–44, 144–146
plastics
    and air pollution, 6
    biodegradable, 68–71
    as hazardous waste, 63–66

as marine pollutants, 42
    nondegradable, 70–71
    photodegradable, 70
    recycling of, 79
    uses for, 64–65
plutonium, 95, 104–105
pollution, 3
    by carbon monoxide, 4
    from car exhaust, 19–20
    by chemicals, 1, 6, 22
    effects on marine animals, 135–137
    marine pollutants, 41–42, 84–88
    from noise, 25–27
    from ozone, 20
    from radiation, 91–106.
    See also air pollution; waste; waste
        disposal; water
polyethylene, 65, 70–71
polymers, 21–22
polystyrene, 65
polyvinyl chloride (PVC), 22
poverty and overpopulation, 151–166
    diseases and malnutrition, 156, 158
    and family planning, 157–159
    and greenhouse effect, 153–155, 166
    improving the status of women,
        162–163
    some solutions, 157–166
Pronczuk deGarbino, Dr. Jenny, 23–
    24

radiation, 2, 3
    from electromagnetic waves, 98
    in food, 95–98
    genetic effects of, 100
    from medical sources, 96–98
    natural sources of, 94–96
    from nuclear power plants, 100–102
    pollution, 91–106
    radioactive waste disposal, 92–94,
        103–106
    safe limits of, 99–100
    ultraviolet, 33–34, 44–45

radioactive elements, 91, 94–97, 99–
    100, 103–105
radium, 95–96, 99
radon, 96
Rainforest Action Network, 121
rain forests, 2
    conservation and management of,
        124–125
    and deforestation, 117–123
    and greenhouse effect, 110
Raven, Peter, 128
Ray, Dixie Lee, 113
recycling, 2, 51, 67, 78–84, 105
    incentives to, 83–84
    methods, 3, 82–84
    responsibility for, 83–84
    resource recovery, 80

Safe Drinking Water Act, 46
salinity, 42–43
scrubbers, 30–31, 34–35, 78, 80, 176
selenium, 42
sewage. *See* waste
Shasta Costa Valley Project, 124–125
Sherman, General William Tecumseh,
    157–158
Silent Spring, 6
Silver Valley, Idaho, 18
sodium nitrite, 22
solar energy, 4, 35, 177–179
solvents, 75
State of the World, 1990, 112
Styrofoam, 65, 66, 72
sulfur dioxide, 22, 29, 31, 33, 35
Superfund program, 72

Thomas, Dr. Lewis, 150
thorium, 95
Three Mile Island, 92, 93, 101, 151
Tickell, Sir Crispin, 104
tidal power, 177, 179
toluol, 63

toxic metals, 78, 135–137.
    See also chemicals: toxic
transportation, 168–175
    automobiles, 169–172
    electric trains, 172–173
    ships, 173–175
trees, 1, 2, 3, 116–117.
    See also deforestation; rain forests
tuna, 134–135

ultraviolet radiation, 33–34
    and the ozone hole, 44–45
Union Carbide, 29
United Nations Population Fund, 151–
    152, 158
uranium, 95, 100
U.S. Department of Energy, 176–177
U.S. Environmental Protection
    Agency (EPA), 9, 48, 59, 71, 73, 137
    and air pollution, 29
    and dioxin, 17
    and lead poisoning, 46
    and radon, 96
    report on toxic substances, 35
U.S. Food and Drug Administration
    (FDA)
    and dioxin levels in fish, 16–17
    and mercury limits, 19
    and PCBs in food, 21
U.S. Forest Service, 124–125
U.S. Marine Mammal Protection Act,
    135
USS Chemicals, 69

Verne, Jules, 179–180
vinyl chloride, 13, 22, 65, 77
viruses, 42, 131, 132
    in dolphins, 135
    in drinking water, 152
vitamins, 7

waste, 56–90
    agricultural, 32

as cause of disease, 137
chemical, 1–2, 23
contamination from landfills, 75
dioxin, 17
household, 61–63
industrial, 57–60, 71
management, 50–51
as marine pollutant, 42
medical, 60–61, 71
military, 58
nonhazardous, 56–57
nuclear, 3, 92
PCBs, 21
plastics, 63, 65, 66
and poverty and overpopulation,
   155–156
and recycling, 78–84
waste stream, 56
waste disposal, 66–67
of asbestos, 11–12, 74
by burying it, 73–76
chemical, 23, 54, 58
by incineration, 30, 76–78
of medical waste, 74
of nuclear waste, 92–94, 103–106,
   177
by ocean dumping, 67, 84–88, 105
by shipping it out, 88–90
by source reduction, 68–73
water, 1, 37–55
and waterborne diseases, 45–46
contaminated drinking water, 152–
   154
contamination from plastics, 65
desalination of, 53
effects of DDT in, 14
and the food chain, 43–44
hydroelectric power, 39
irrigation systems, 42–43
PCBs in, 21, 42
protection laws, 50–51

radioactive contamination of, 96,
   106
recycling, 51
rights, 52–53
and salinity, 42–43
and waste contamination, 57, 84–88
water-saving methods, 54–55
wetlands, 47–49, 132
whales and whaling, 132–134, 138–
   139
wildlife, 1, 126–150
acclimation of, 128, 129
birds, 66, 140–141
causes of extinction, 126–129
conservation of, 150
crustaceans, 137–138
and DDT, 14–15, 136, 140–141
and deforestation, 122
dolphins, 134–135
effect of logging on, 140
elephants and ivory, 138–139
fish and fishing, 16–17, 21, 47, 51,
   136
and habitat destruction, 139–140
insects, 3, 141–144
interdependency, 130
interrelationship, 130–131
and PCBs, 21
✓ and polluted water, 37
protection of, 147–150
tuna, 134–135
whales and whaling, 132–134, 138–
   139
wind power, 35, 177
World Health Organization, 32–33,
   52–53, 97, 111
Worldwatch Institute, 51, 111–112,
   124–125, 152, 155, 169–170,
   177

zinc, 136